Cityscape
Ben Johnson's Liverpool

Edited by Ann Bukantas

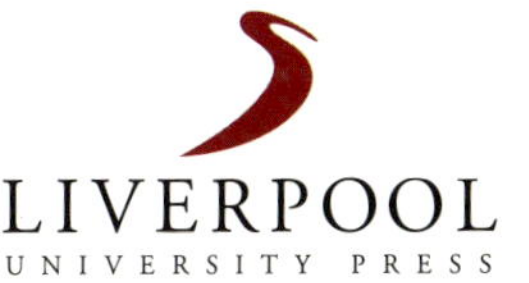

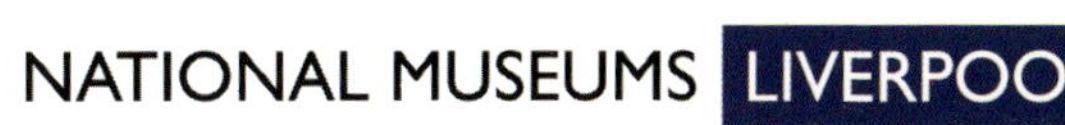

LIVERPOOL
UNIVERSITY PRESS

NATIONAL MUSEUMS LIVERPOOL

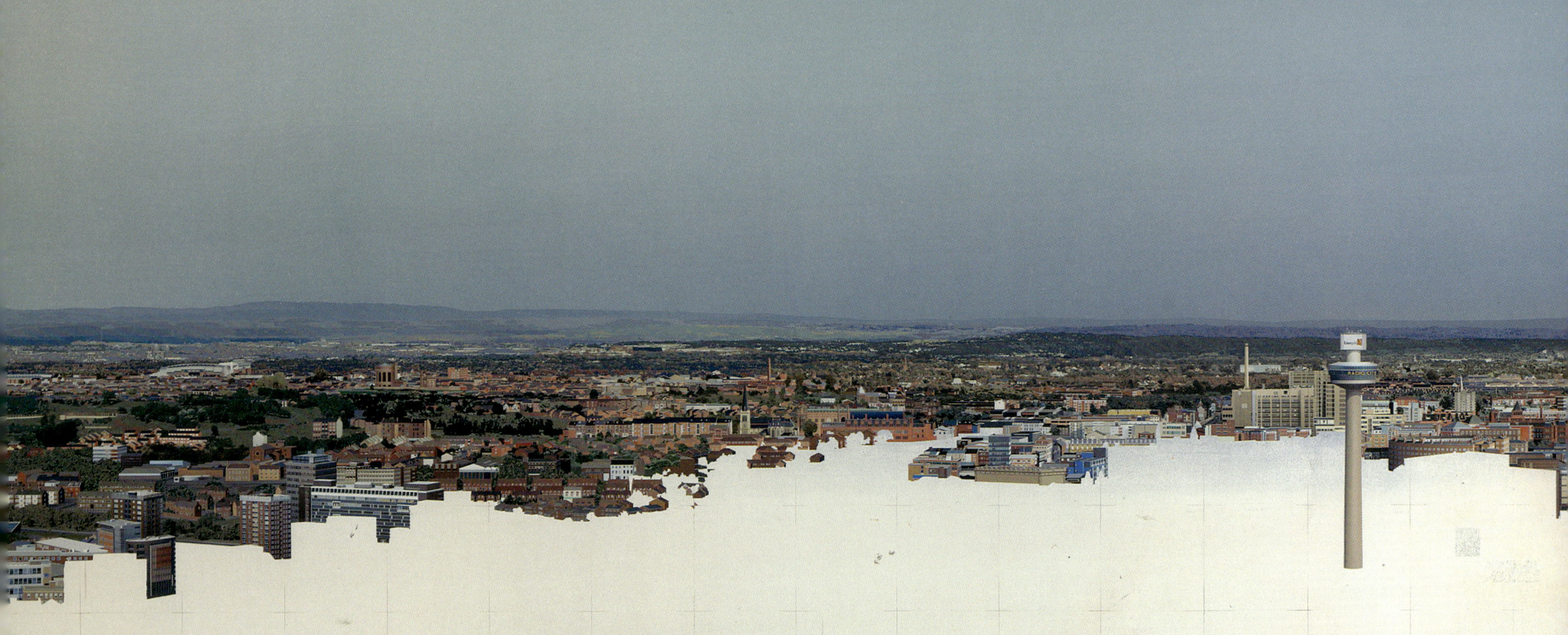

First published 2008 by

Liverpool University Press
4 Cambridge Street
Liverpool
L69 7ZU

and

National Museums Liverpool
127 Dale Street
Liverpool
L2 2JH

British Library Cataloguing-in-Publication data
A British Library CIP record is available

ISBN 978-1-84631-157-4

Designed by AW @ www.axisgraphicdesign.co.uk
Printed and bound by EBS, Verona

Ben Johnson's Liverpool

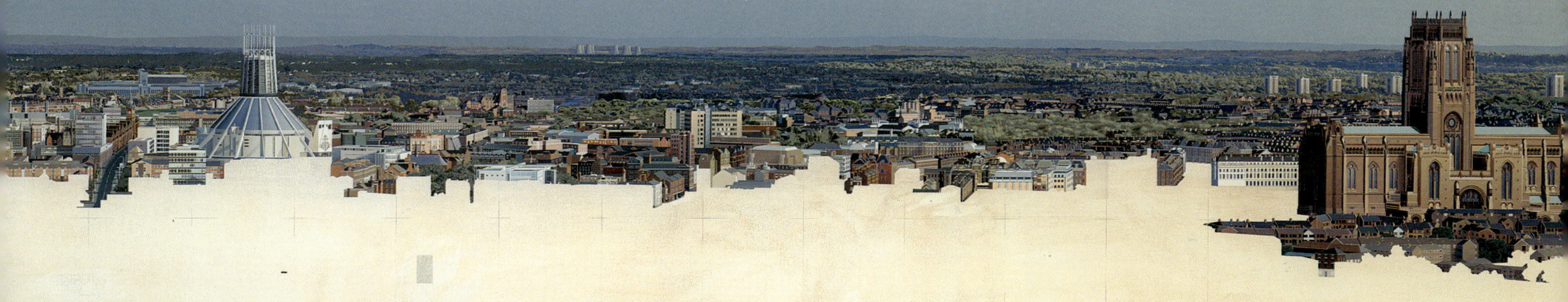

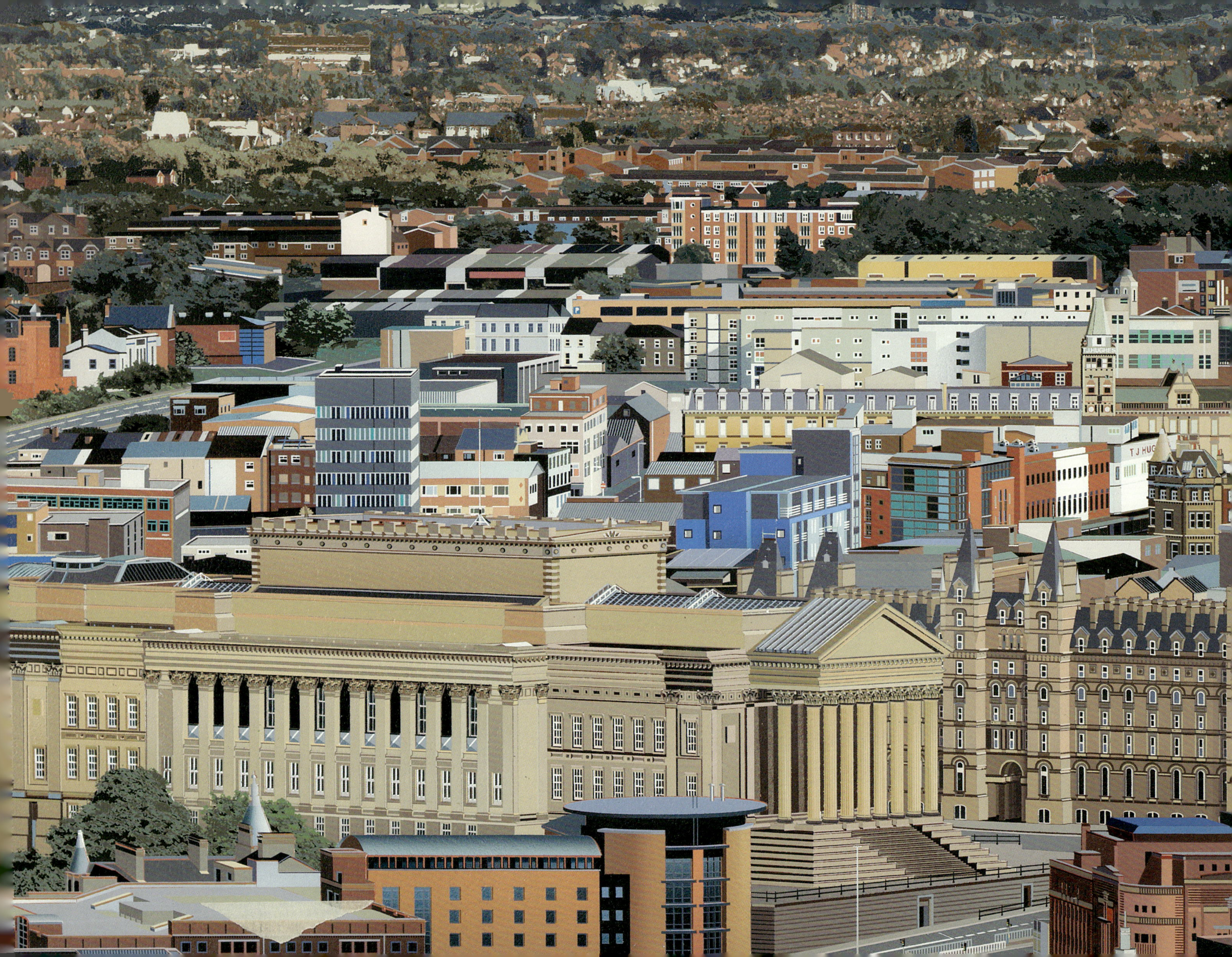
TJ HUGHES
T J HUG

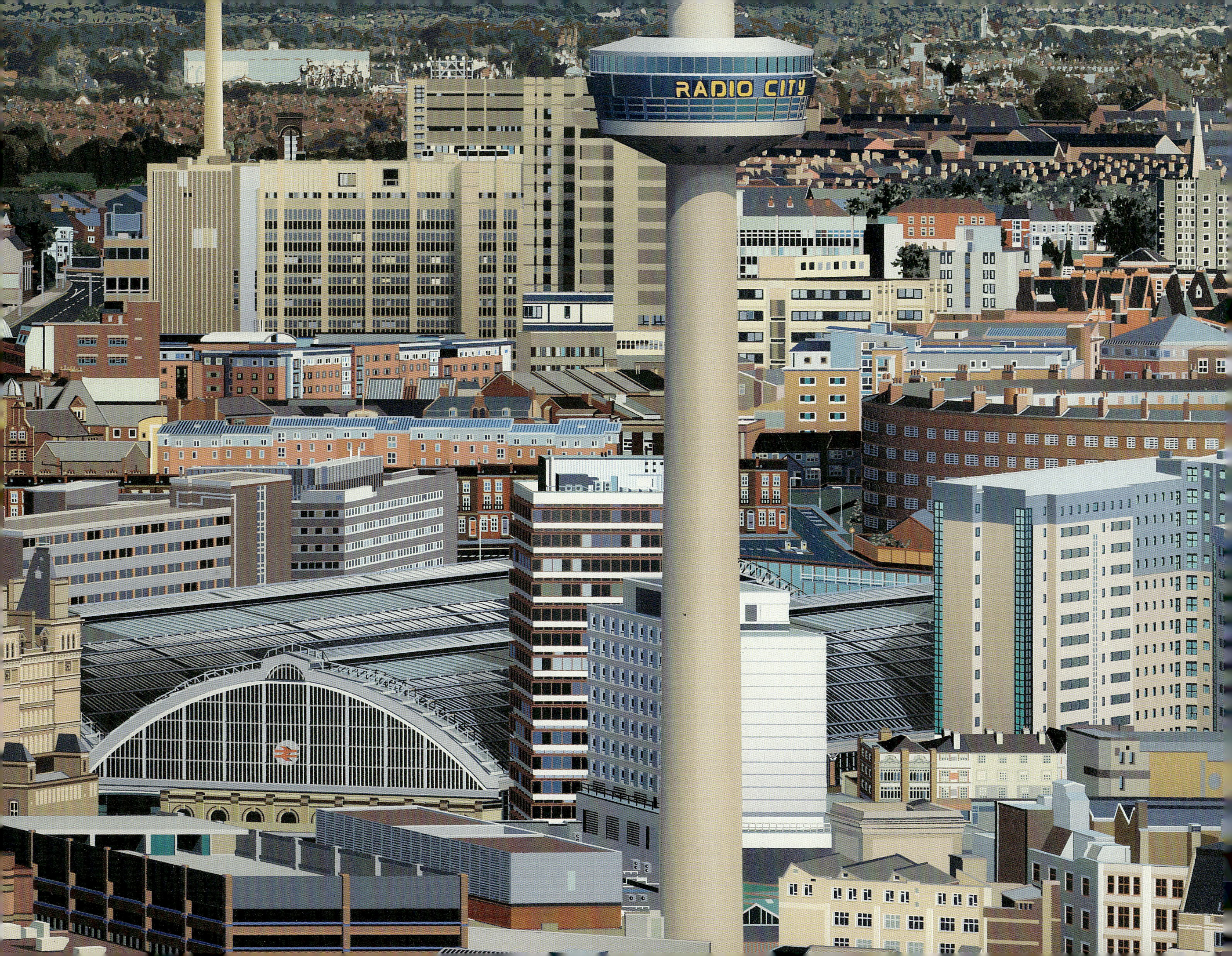

RADIO CITY

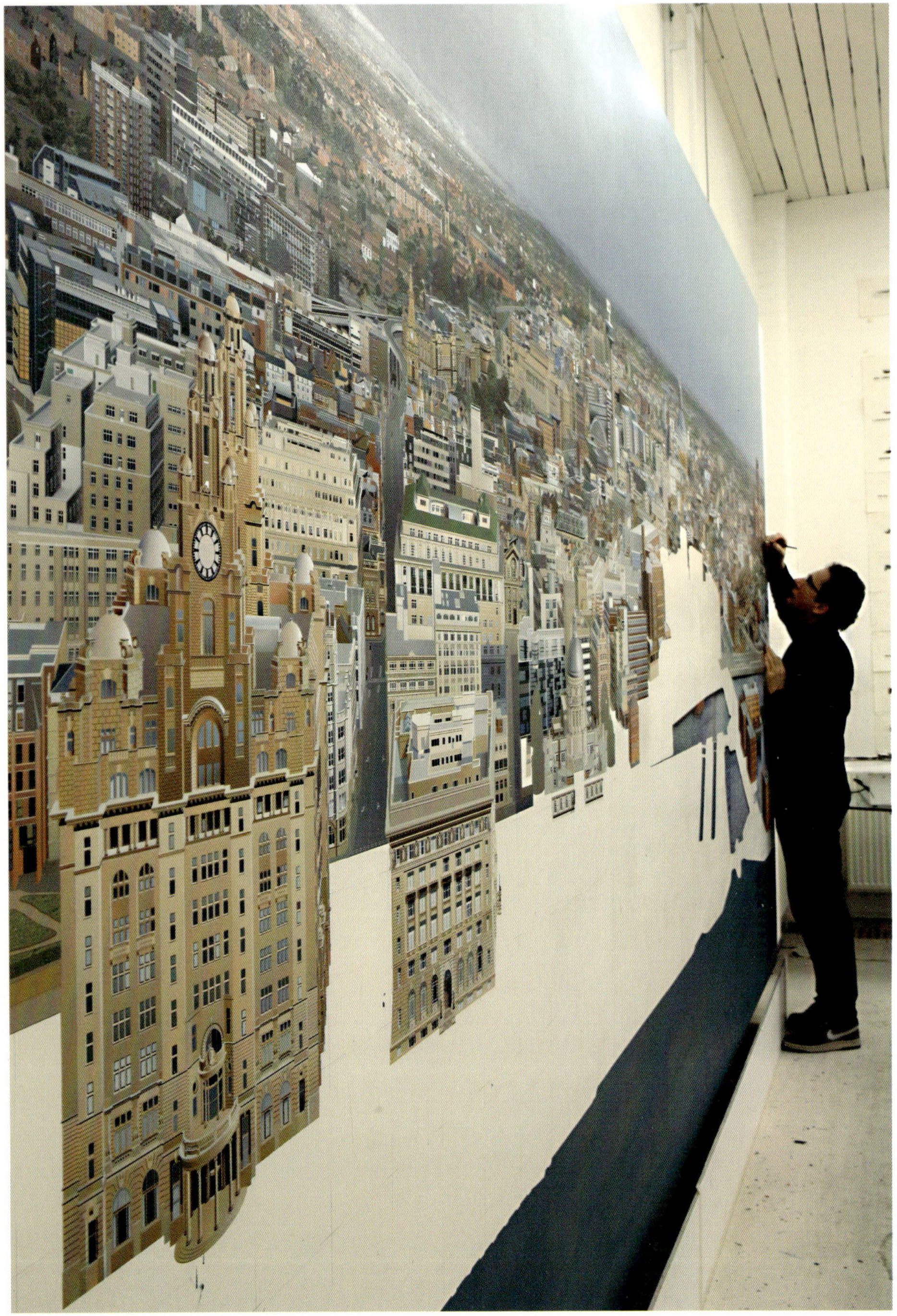

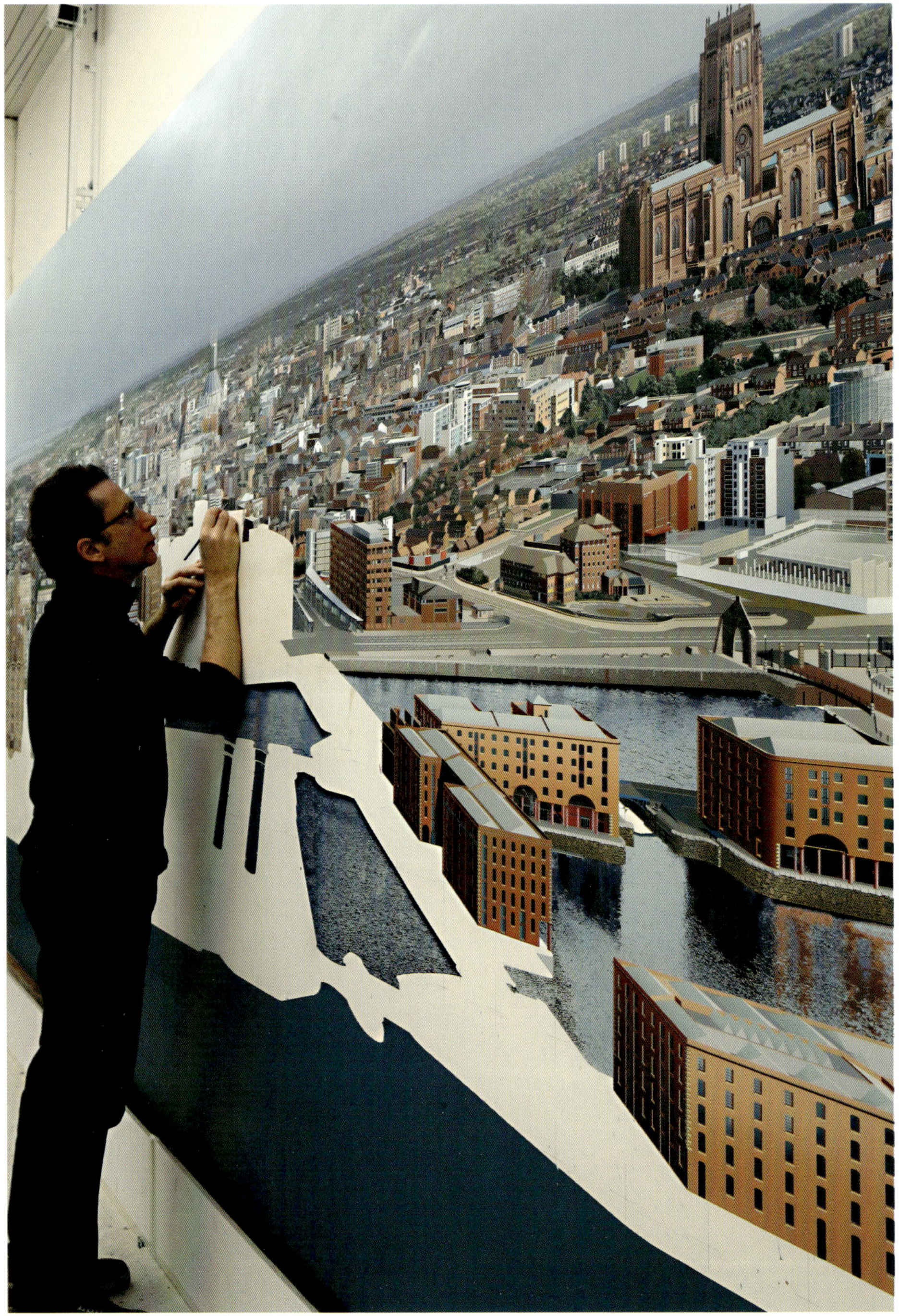

Foreword

Dr David Fleming OBE
Director
National Museums Liverpool

As soon as we knew at National Museums Liverpool (NML) that the city was to become the European Capital of Culture in 2008, we started planning a host of activities and events which would ensure that the year is a special one, particularly for local people.

It wasn't long before the prospect of a Ben Johnson commission was mooted. I remember the first time it was introduced. I listened to a patient explanation from our art staff about Ben, what the commission might be, and how appropriate it would be for the city to have a 'portrait' of itself to mark this momentous year. When the presentation began I thought, 'This sounds interesting – but it isn't going to be cheap'.

As their talk proceeded the project began to sound more and more ambitious and spectacular. I resisted the temptation to interrupt the unfolding tale of artistic merit and community value by asking, 'How much?' It wasn't until right at the end that I learned the precise nature of what was to become a new fundraising challenge for NML, but by then I was so enthusiastic about the commission that I felt it was an obvious commitment for us to make. We were quick to commit to such an exciting and appropriate project.

Ben confirmed that he was both available and excited by the prospect of creating this work inspired by a city he knows well and loves. The project was up and running.

More than three years have passed since then. Today, Ben Johnson's painting, *The Liverpool Cityscape*, is an extraordinary work of art. It is on a scale commensurate both with the city's remarkable history and with its dramatic skyline. It offers a new perspective on Liverpool which will entrance local people and visitors alike. It is all the more exciting that Ben finished the Cityscape here in Liverpool, at the Walker Art Gallery. The painting will become an iconic part of NML's collections, initially on show at the Walker but later to find a permanent home in the new Museum of Liverpool. There it will be a 'must see' element for anyone interested in stories of the city they think they know.

Indeed, the Cityscape opens up, literally, a new vista on Liverpool. It highlights some familiar sights but also makes the familiar unfamiliar, causing the viewer to re-engage with the city's topography.

I know this because many people have glimpsed the painting in progress, and without exception they have all been astonished at what they have seen – a view which they thought they knew backwards, but which is illuminated anew by the techniques of Ben and his remarkable team.

I wish to thank a number of people who made this project possible. First and foremost, thanks to Ben and his dedicated team: Richard Gibson, Sheila Johnson, Christopher Raymond, Ben Wakely, Richard Wade, Hannah Waldron, Philip Morgan, Charlie Johnson, Sarah Sharma and James Maj. Thanks also to the many others who contributed. They have been a pleasure to work with, and have co-operated in every way imaginable to help NML ensure that the project is a successful one.

Thanks particularly to our funders, notably Professor Phil Redmond CBE and Mrs Alexis Redmond, whose early involvement and enthusiasm convinced us that we had a winner on our hands, and to co-commissioners Liverpool's Culture Company who also gave early support. Others who have supported the commission include David M. Robinson Ltd, Liverpool Vision, Northwest Regional Development Agency, Ethel Austin Properties Group, Barbara A. McVey and Rensburg Sheppards Investment Management. The related exhibition has been sponsored by the University of Liverpool.

And thanks must also go to the many NML staff involved, particularly to Ann Bukantas who first came forward with the proposal for the commission and who has seen the project through to a triumphant conclusion, and to our fundraising and exhibitions teams. Many local people and organisations – too numerous to name – have also helped Ben in his research, and a special thanks is extended to them too.

This painting is a gift to the citizens of Liverpool from THEIR museum service, to mark a very special year. It is destined to become one of those rare museum items which everyone sees, everyone remembers, and everyone takes friends, children and grandchildren to see again and again. All else around us will change, but Ben Johnson's painting, *The Liverpool Cityscape*, will be here in the city forever, capturing Liverpool at a turning point in its fortunes, 2008.

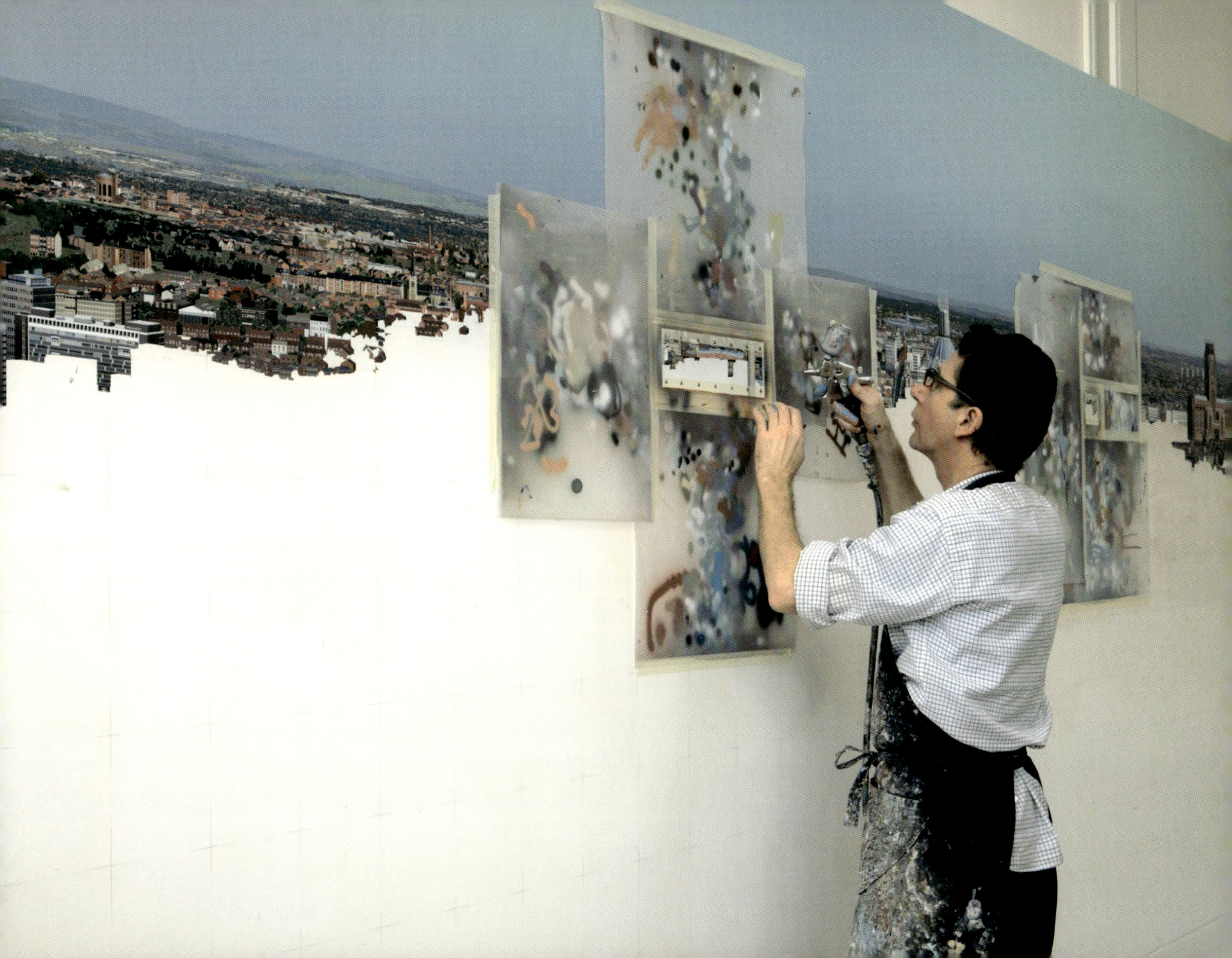

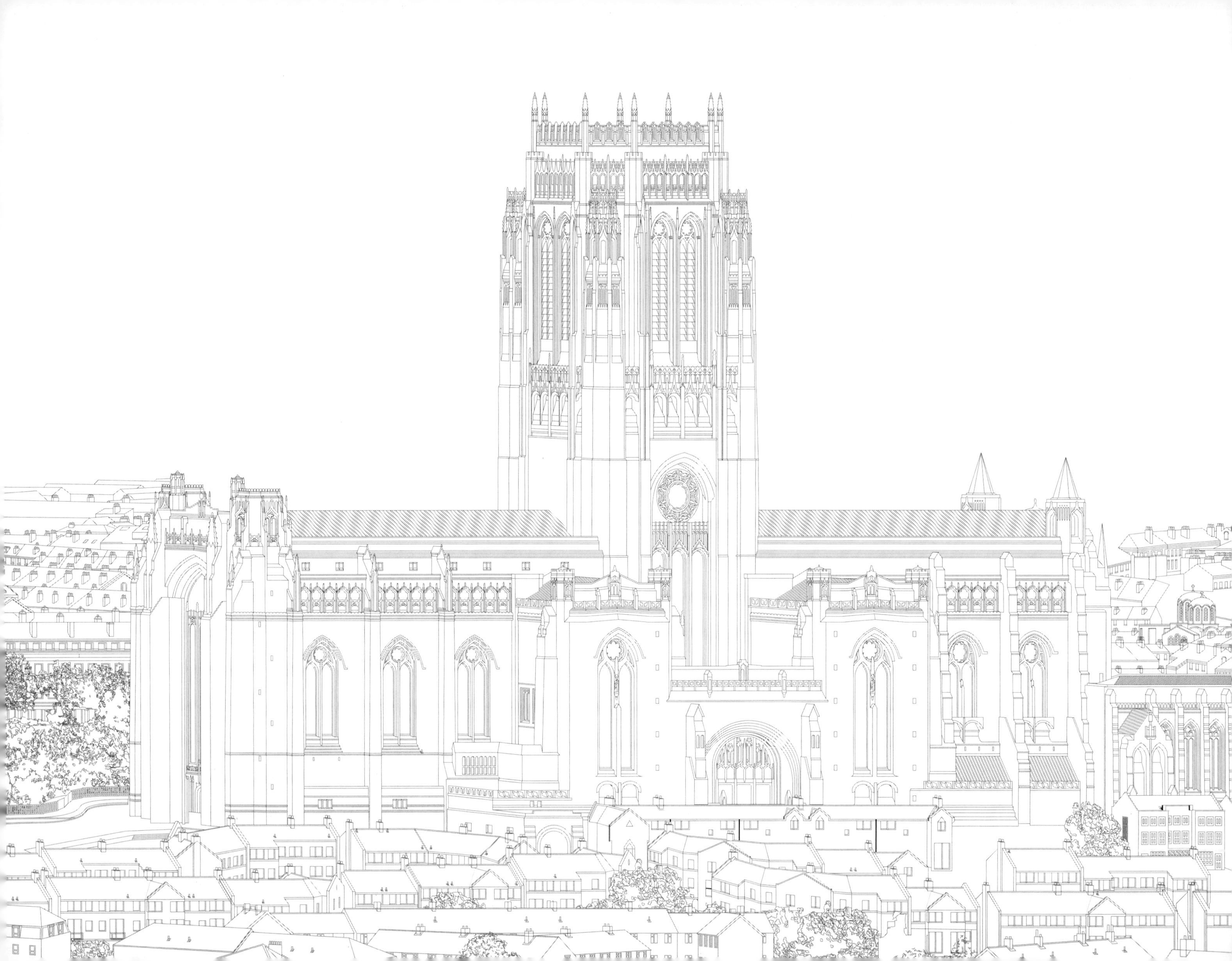

Introduction

Sir Norman Foster

For me, life and art are inextricably linked – I cannot imagine living in a world without the aesthetic 'lift' that art can give us. Ideally art and architecture should go hand in hand. Over the years, I have collaborated with many artists. At its best, that experience can be both pleasurable and stimulating. It can also open up new architectural possibilities.

Ben Johnson is an artist who has been concerned with architecture almost from the moment he started painting. But it would be wrong to suggest that what he does is simply to depict buildings or cities. Instead he captures their spirit. As an architect, I have always been amazed by his uncanny ability to sum up a building in a single image, to distil its essence. Similarly, with cities he can create on canvas a view that represents perfectly our mental image of the place, even though he might have manipulated its topography, or used artistic licence to capture an idealised view.

As European Capital of Culture 2008, Liverpool's arts scene is energised and invigorated as never before. Ben Johnson's panoramic portrait of Liverpool is part of this phenomenon – both a celebration of the city's artistic status and an historical document in its own right. Importantly, it was also conceived as a catalyst for other community art events and projects during 2008. 'Events', as Ben Johnson himself says, 'that put the people back into the painting: an important factor, as my city is unpopulated.'

As you would expect, all the city's significant existing buildings are portrayed. You might argue that the camera could do that equally well. But then the artist's imagination takes over. He includes projects that are designed and due to be completed in 2008, and landmark buildings upon which work has started. In that sense, he paints the dynamic of a city in progress rather than one frozen in time.

The totality is an iconic image – one that you can carry readily in your mind's eye. Yet close up, one sees that it is composed of many thousands of exquisitely detailed miniatures, where the same loving care is applied to the lowliest industrial warehouse as it is to the loftiest cathedral. There are other twists and turns too. The city is bathed in light, which is even and strong, suggesting a midsummer's day. Yet look closely and you see that the streets are empty, and the city is still, as it might be at dawn.

The painting is a contemporary interpretation of the Classical tradition, in which myth and reality are interwoven. Artists such as Canaletto or Turner would have understood immediately the spirit at play here. It has a dreamlike quality. It is both a moment in time and a timeless exploration – a wonderful achievement in every sense.

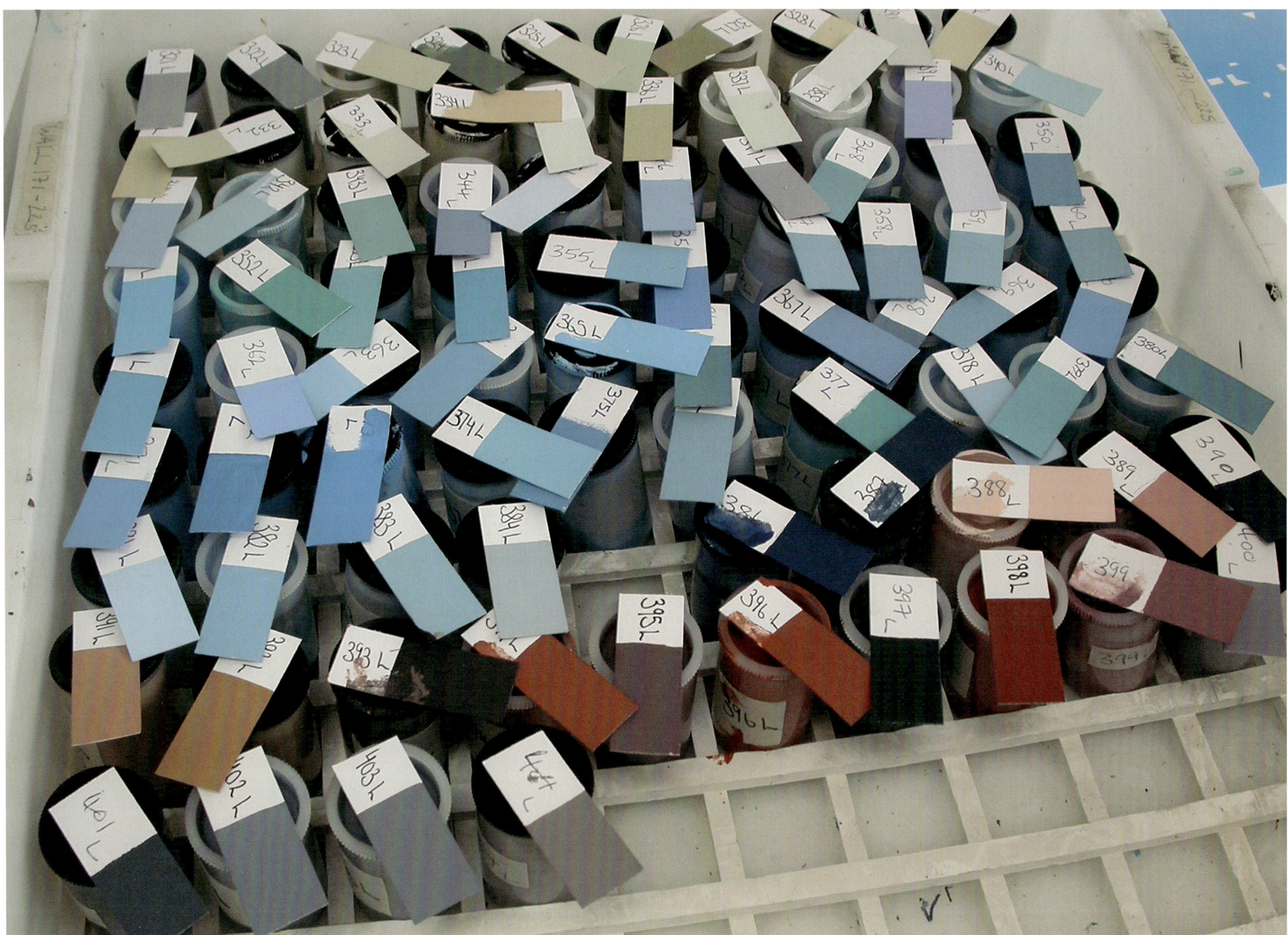

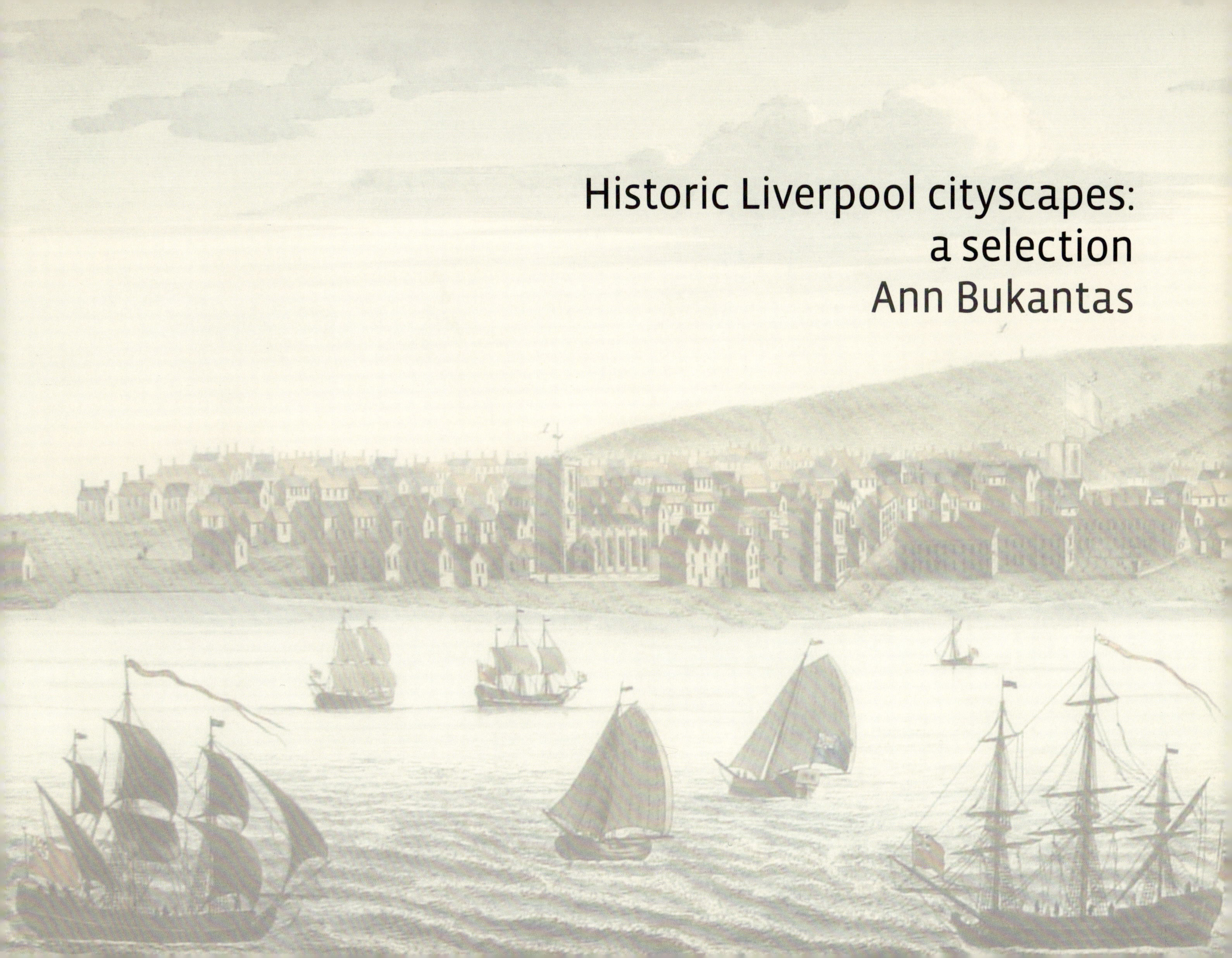

Historic Liverpool cityscapes:
a selection
Ann Bukantas

In common with Britain's other major towns and cities, Liverpool attracted the attention of many artists, both locals and visitors, whose aim was to produce a visual record of the locality. The term 'panorama' is sometimes applied to the more extensive of these views, but they were not the vast, realistic circular panoramas that attracted large crowds in the nineteenth century. Rather, they were an array of paintings, drawings, maps and prints created for the walls of private collectors or galleries, for inclusion in books and periodicals or for distribution by a network of publishers and dealers. Whatever the end result, the artists shared a common goal: to describe Liverpool's swiftly expanding port and townscape. Indirectly they reveal the progressive growth of its population and its fortunes through its built environment. Their work reflected pride in the mounting importance of Liverpool in the mercantile world. This was particularly true in the nineteenth century, a period of rapid growth for the town.

Early views, produced without reference to maps, were partly dependent upon artistic invention but stand as a valid and valuable record of Liverpool prior to its expansion. Into the eighteenth century, the scenes were more topographical or descriptive, such as the 1728 prospect by Samuel and Nathaniel Buck. These views combined artistic merit with a better understanding of the town's layout. A survey of Liverpool by John Chadwick in 1725 permitted this improved level of accuracy. Into the nineteenth century the line between the cartographers' maps and the artists' representations started to blur, and by the mid-nineteenth century, when the 'bird's-eye' views flourished, the artists' images had effectively become three-dimensional maps. These would gradually be outpaced by the camera and the rise of aerial photography.

Liverpool's cityscape maintained its attraction into the twentieth century. In particular, large schemes to record Merseyside, embracing artists, photographers and film-makers, continued in the decades after the Second World War. Ben Johnson's painting *The Liverpool Cityscape* is the most recent addition to this ambitious lineage. A selection of some of the most comparable and significant of the historic works from the collections of National Museums Liverpool and the Liverpool Record Office are introduced here.

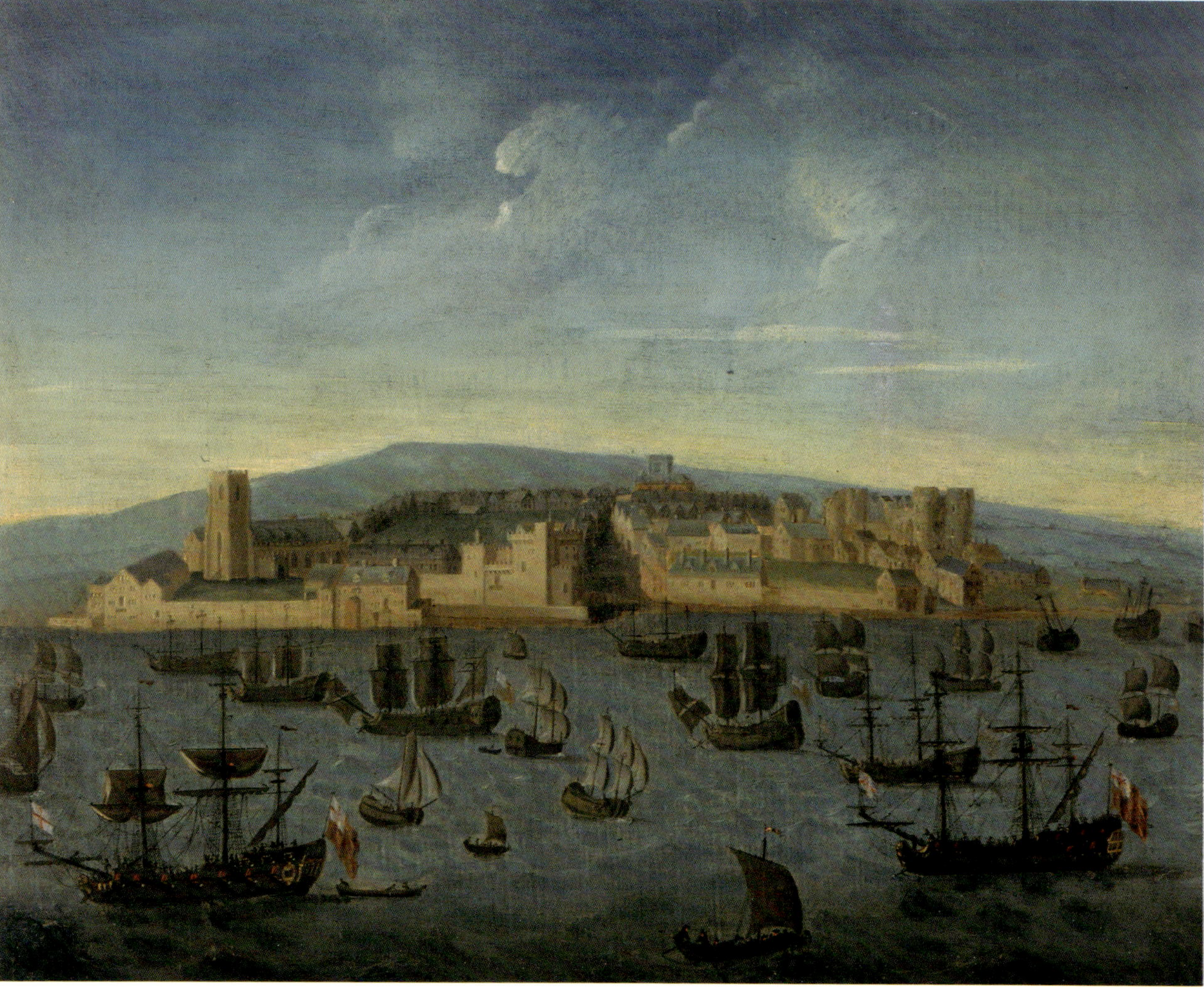

This is almost certainly the earliest painting of Liverpool. In the eighteenth century it was owned by the Peters family of Liverpool and it is often referred to as the 'Peters painting'. It shows the main part of the waterfront and town in about 1680 with a wealth of trading, coastal and local river vessels on the water. Liverpool is in its compact, medieval form, just prior to its rapid development. The town nestles between the Pool – a natural, sheltered harbour – and the river Mersey. A number of key buildings dominate. To the left is St Nicholas's chapel (now, after centuries of rebuilding, Our Lady and St Nicholas). The central castellated building is the Tower, the Earl of Derby's former town house, around three centuries old by 1680. Water Street, which is prominent in Ben Johnson's view, appears to the right of the Tower. On the opposite corner of Water Street, with its four chimneys, is the Custom House. The dilapidated thirteenth-century castle stands to the right of the townscape. Breaking the line of the far horizon is the tower of the Town Hall, in almost the same position as its modern successor. The influence of this painting on subsequent artists and cartographers was enduring. An engraving of the Peters painting, made by John Eyes in 1766, was the inspiration for numerous copies made over the centuries.

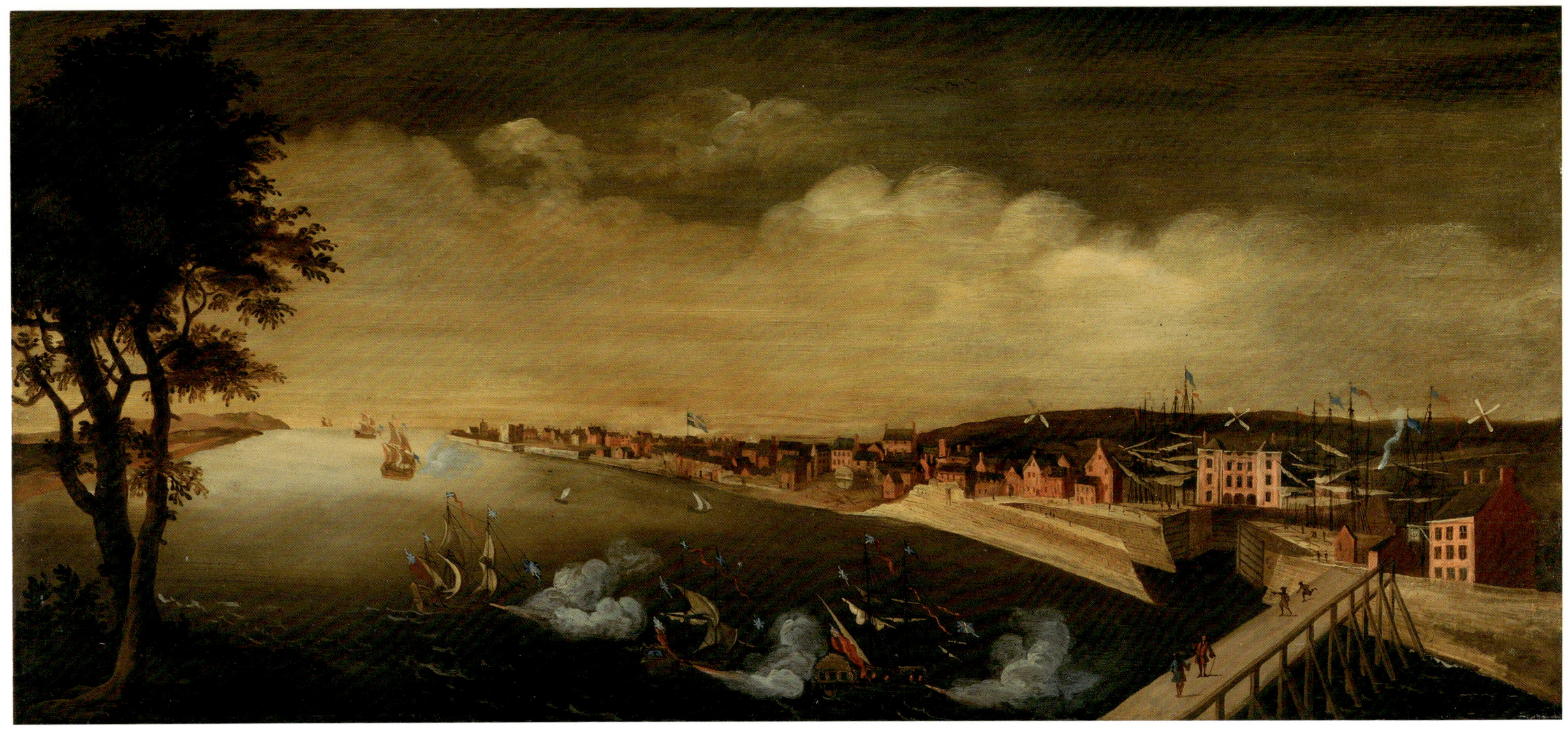

Prospect of Liverpool, about 1725

Artist unknown
Merseyside Maritime Museum (National Museums Liverpool)
MMM.2001.8
Oil on panel: 66.5 x 147.8 cm

The town's expansion since the 1680 view was painted is apparent here. This imaginary and elevated scene, probably created by a travelling 'journeyman' artist, is thought to be the earliest representation of Liverpool's first dock, opened in 1715. The dock's prominence, dominating the right-hand side of the painting, reflects the centre of the town's commercial development in the first quarter of the eighteenth century. At its head stands the new, brick-built Custom House, with an inn on the extreme right. Behind them, windmills stand on the higher ground. A wooden jetty protruding into the foreground is used as a striking compositional device, upon which bystanders gather to watch ships fire a salute. Shipbuilding activity can be seen in the open space along the shoreline. Further along, a large flag indicates the position of the Town Hall and Exchange. By 1725 the castle had been demolished and, of the older landmarks, only St Nicholas's and the Tower remained. The opposite river bank is the Wirral peninsula.

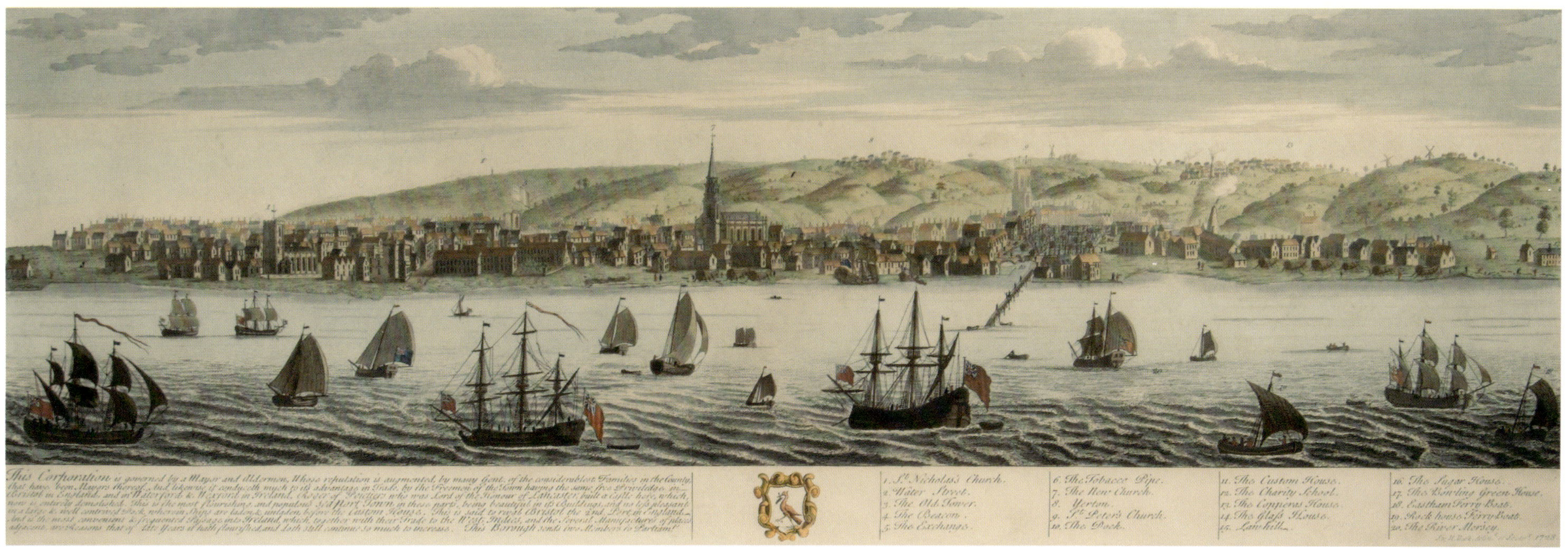

The South West Prospect of Liverpoole in the County Palatine of Lancaster, 1728
Samuel (1696–1779) and Nathaniel Buck (working 1724–after 1753)
Liverpool Record Office, Liverpool Libraries
LIC 228
Engraving: 20.5 x 70.8 cm

In this well-known engraved view of 1728 the developing town is dominated by two large new churches, St Peter's (completed 1704) and St George's. Construction work on the latter began in 1727 but the church was not consecrated until 1734. It appears as 'the New Church' (7) on the image. Like Ben Johnson, the artists probably worked with the architect's drawings to complete the building, thus depicting modern progress in the town. Liverpool's first enclosed dock is prominent in the centre. Also included is the landing pier from which ferry boats embarked. Two boats in the foreground are on their way to Eastham and Rock Ferry. Glass making, sugar refining and shipbuilding are also evident. The town remains quite compact, surrounded by hills. In the north, the still separate village of Everton stands on one of these, while St James's Mount is to the south. The brothers Samuel and Nathaniel Buck were prolific topographical draughtsmen who produced over 80 engraved views of British towns and cities.

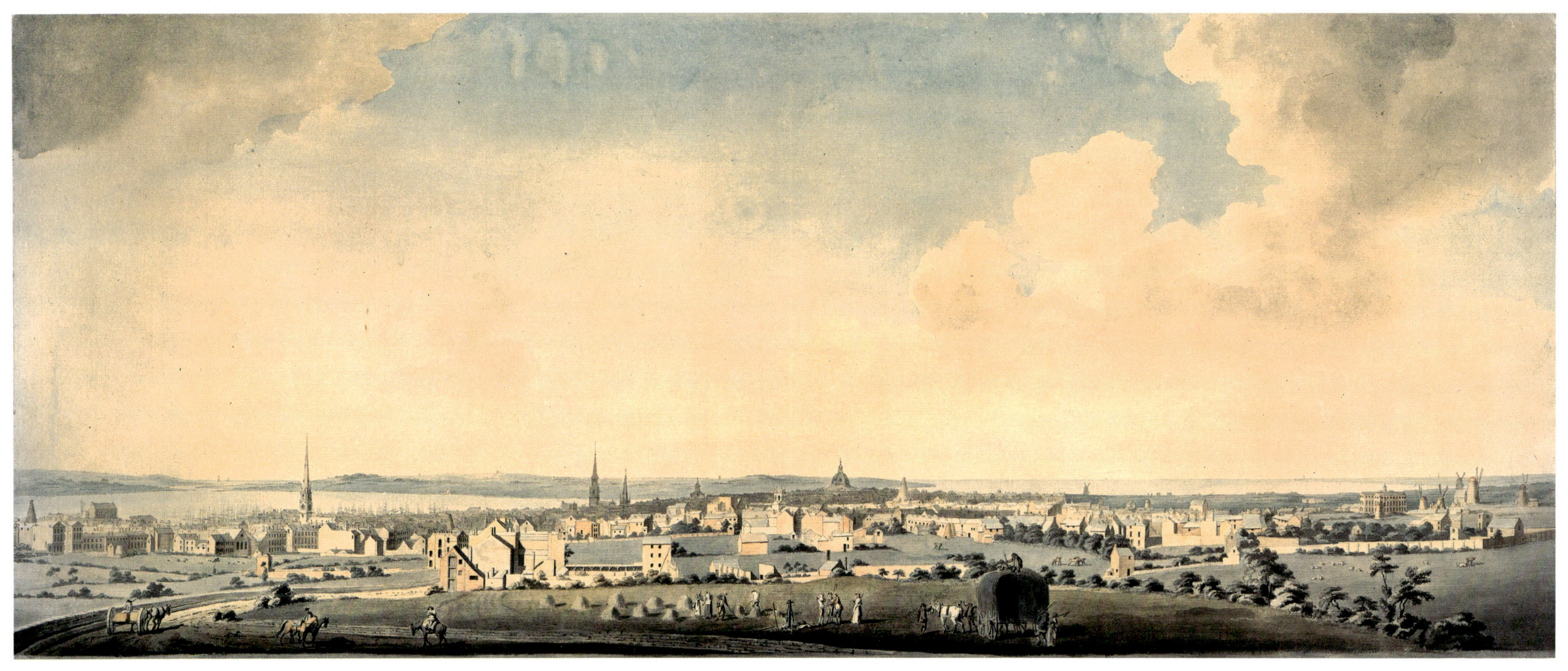

Liverpool from the Bowling Green, 1769

Michael Angelo Rooker (1746–1801)
Walker Art Gallery (National Museums Liverpool)
WAG 8654
Watercolour on paper: 30.5 x 76cm

This is one of a pair of panoramas made in conjunction with a new survey of Liverpool by the publisher and historian George Perry, begun in 1768. Prints of Rooker's two watercolours were engraved by the artist's father and published in 1770. The viewpoint is similar, though far less elevated, to that taken over a century later by Brewer and Wyllie in their 1885 bird's-eye view (see page 21). The bowling green mentioned in Rooker's title was in the town's Upper Duke Street area. The buildings, from left to right, include the churches of St Thomas, St George and St Nicholas. The Old Town Hall is the lower dome and St Paul's church the larger one. Over to the right is the Infirmary, standing on the site now occupied by St George's Hall. The windmills are in the Lime Street and Islington area, taking advantage of the higher land.

Panoramic view of Liverpool, 1847
Published by Ackermann & Co.
Liverpool Record Office, Liverpool Libraries
LIC 901
Engraving: 54 x 81 cm

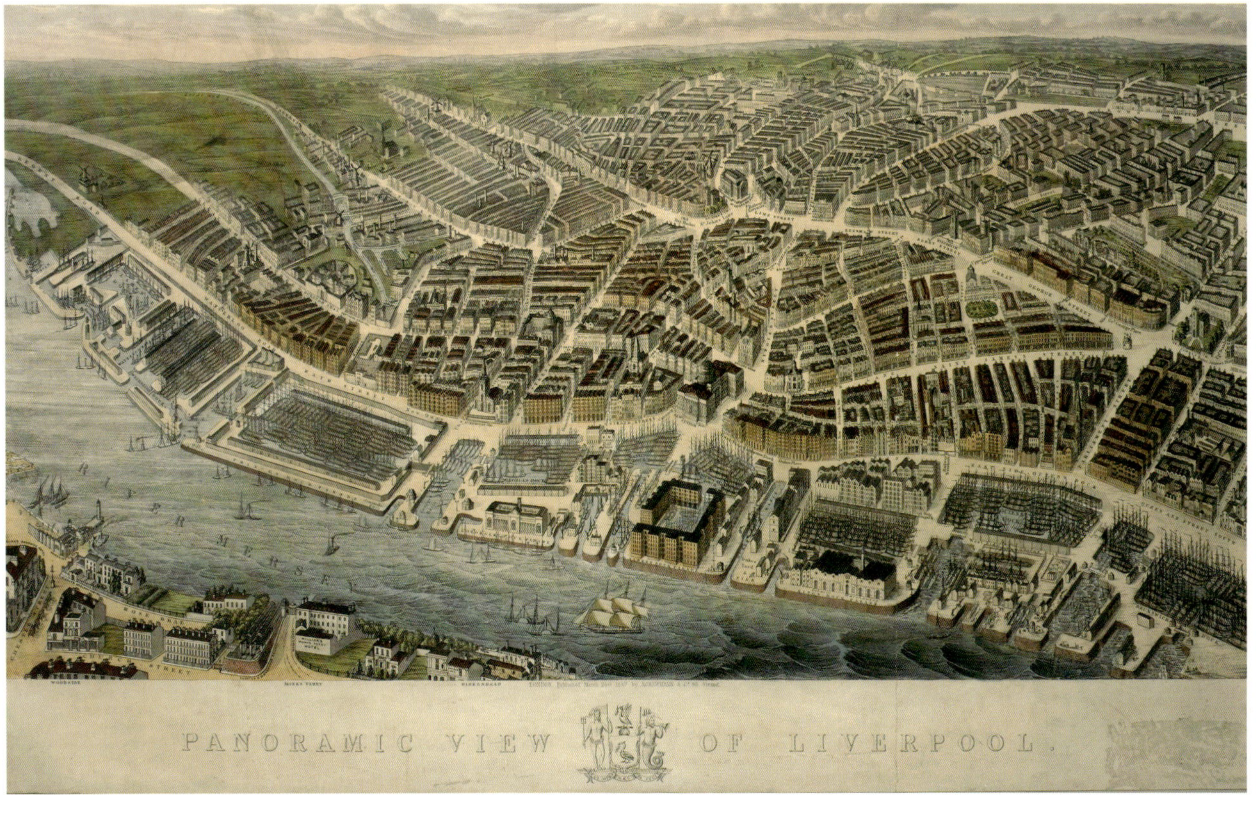

This is undoubtedly one of the most attractive of the numerous nineteenth-century views of Liverpool. Probably assisted by a balloon ascent, the panorama's artist marshals the waterfront and streets into an orderly formation to present the town as a carefully labelled three-dimensional map, with the Birkenhead shore facing. Ordnance Survey maps were a possible reference source. Despite the artist recording a substantial spread of agricultural land on the outskirts of Liverpool, the scene still highlights the enormous increase in the area covered by buildings and docks compared with the earlier views. Almost 300 acres of enclosed docks were built along seven miles of waterfront. The density of industry and habitation was great, with a population of some 340,000, excluding the suburb-dwellers. Of particular note in this view is the Liverpool–Manchester Railway, opened in 1830. Its route can be traced from the 'Railway Entrance' tunnel on Lime Street to its reappearance in the top right-hand corner of the panorama, above Crown Street. The path of the Leeds–Liverpool canal, entering the town from the opposite direction at the end of its 127-mile journey, is also clear. St George's Hall is included, even though it would not be complete for a further seven years. The first public baths and washhouses in the country were opened in Liverpool in 1842. The public baths building stands proudly at the centre of the line of docks on George's Dock Parade. The panorama's publishers were the well-established Ackermann & Co. of London, but the artist remains unrecorded.

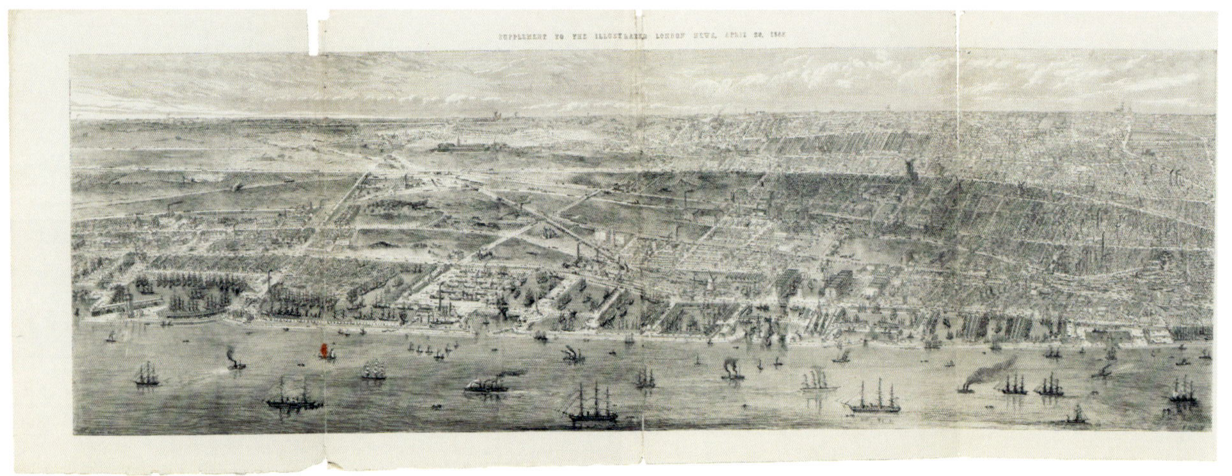

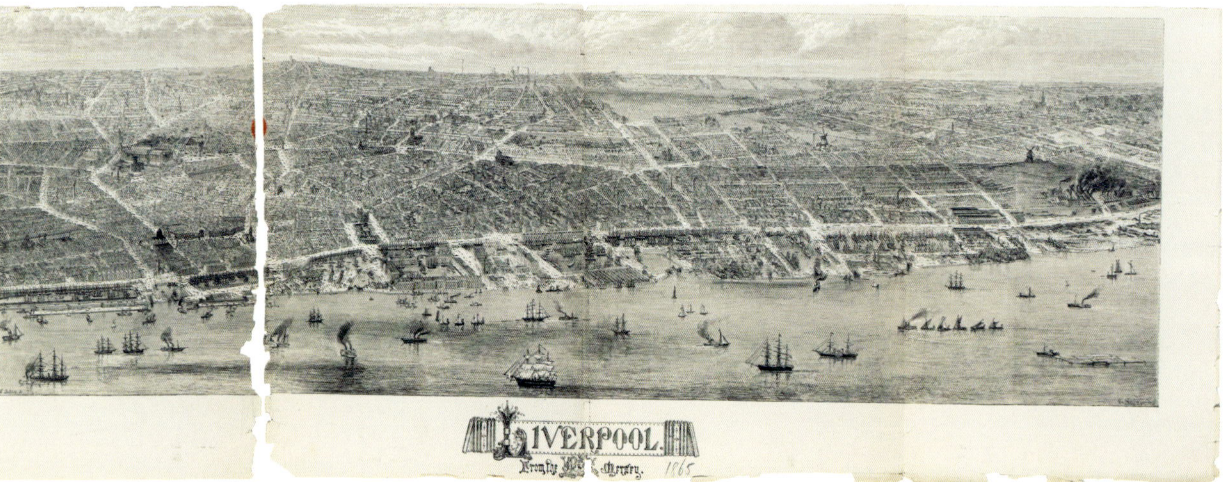

Liverpool from the Mersey, 1865
Mason Jackson (c.1820–1903) and Thomas Sulman (active 1855–1900)
Merseyside Maritime Museum (National Museums Liverpool)
MMM.1972.231.25
Engraving

Jackson and Sulman's remarkable panorama of *Liverpool from the Mersey* was included as a supplement to the 29 April 1865 edition of the *Illustrated London News*. Owing to its extraordinary length – over six feet (1.8 metres) – it was divided into two sections, one printed above the other. An accompanying article about the town's history was carried in the main paper. That Liverpool was given such prominence is a testament to the national importance of the port. As well as revealing the vast expansion of Liverpool's built environment, this view demonstrates how busy the Mersey was, with a wide variety of vessels. Miles of docks are encompassed, presenting an entire working environment including the graving docks, ship repair and timber under tow. Features of the Bootle end (upper section) include the Salisbury Dock clock tower and the vast Stanley Dock warehouses. At the Liverpool end (lower section) George's Dock is still present; this was not drained until the end of the century, creating the Pier Head and the site of the Three Graces.

Windmills, which were used for pumping water and grinding both foodstuffs and minerals for industry, form a distinctive feature of this vista. There were a considerable number up until 1900, with a few even surviving into the twentieth century. The artist here was Thomas Sulman, an architectural draughtsman who produced several panoramic views. He was taught by Dante Gabriel Rossetti at the Working Men's College in London. The print's engraver, Mason Jackson, became art editor of the *Illustrated London News* in 1860.

Bird's-eye view of Liverpool, as seen from a balloon, 1885
Henry William Brewer (d.1903) and William Lionel Wyllie
(1851–1931)
Merseyside Maritime Museum (National Museums Liverpool)
Engraving

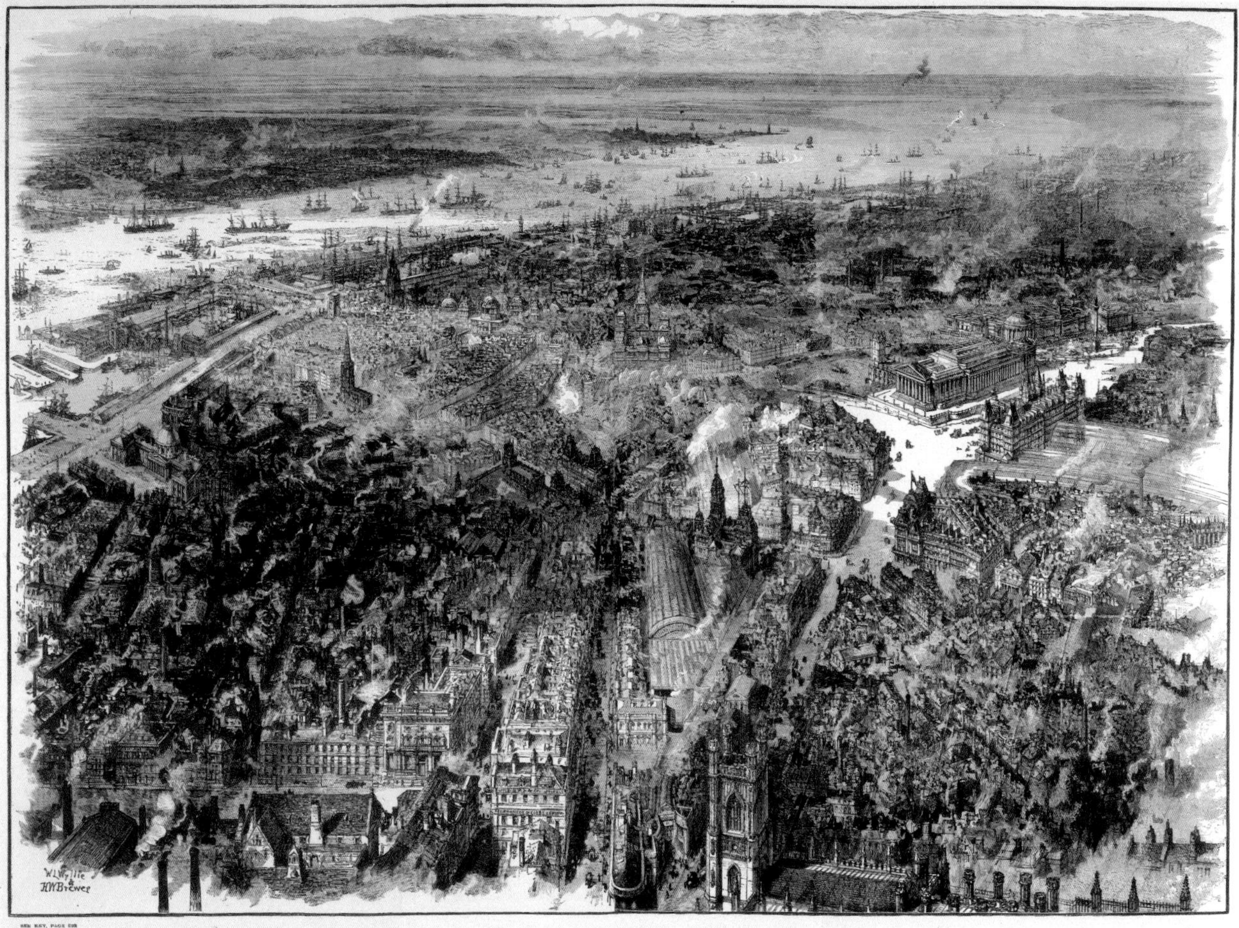

BIRD'S·EYE VIEW OF LIVERPOOL, AS SEEN FROM A BALLOON, 1885

This view of Liverpool – granted city status by Royal Charter in 1880 – looks out towards the Mersey and the Wirral coast. It was reproduced as a supplement to the 22 August 1885 edition of the *Graphic*, a London-based illustrated weekly newspaper. A key listing the scene's main landmarks and a critical commentary on Liverpool's layout by Brewer appeared in the main section of the paper. There, he advocated protecting Liverpool's open spaces, including the plateau around St George's Hall, seen towards the right of this view. In 1884–6 a competition was underway for a new Cathedral, to be built alongside on the site of St John's church, visible here to the left of the Hall. Brewer argued this would 'injure the effect' of St George's Hall and must have rejoiced when the project collapsed in 1888. Brewer and Wyllie's view shows the central part of the town. It was taken from a spot south-east of St Luke's church (which appears in the foreground of the scene) and was based on sketches made upon the spot. Like Ben Johnson, the artist climbed up various tall buildings, including church towers, to make his sketches. A balloon was also employed. Brewer was an architectural and interior painter from London. Wyllie was a marine painter and maritime illustrator for the *Graphic*, accomplished at sketching under difficult conditions.

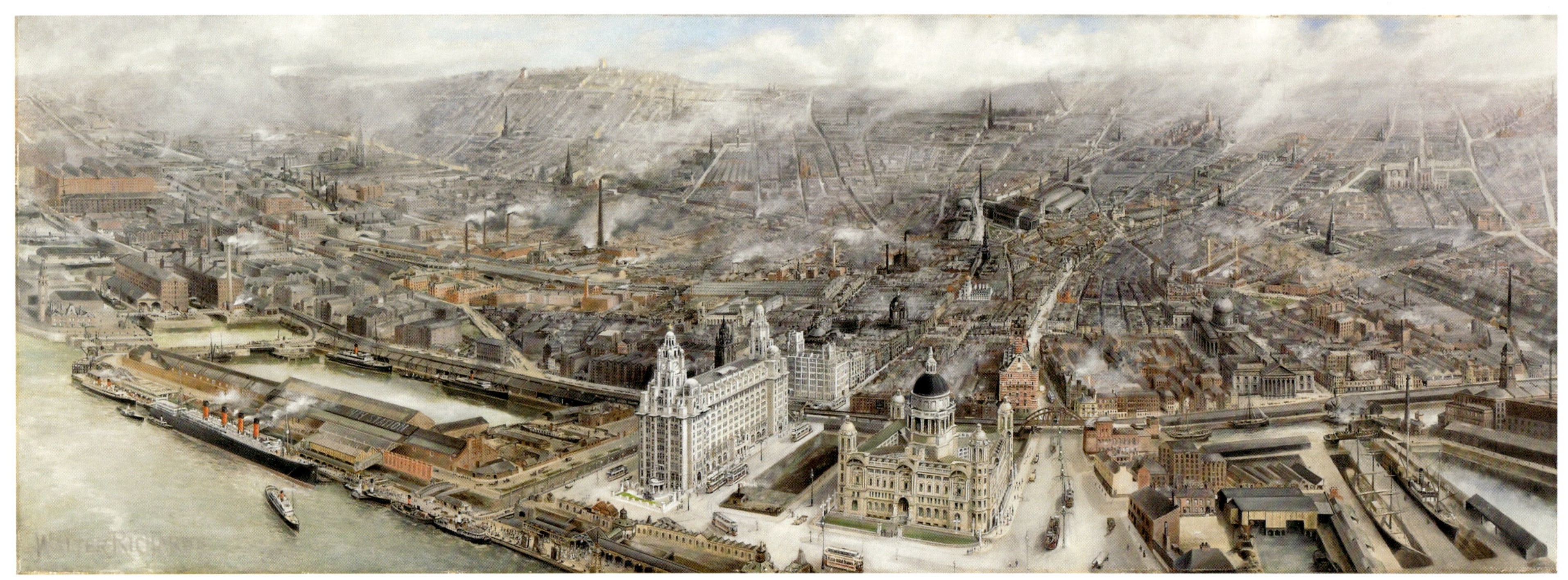

Modern Liverpool, 1907
Walter Richards
Merseyside Maritime Museum (National Museums Liverpool)
MMM.2007.31
Oil on canvas: 61.5 x 173 cm

Walter Richards' detailed view shows the Edwardian city at the height of its prosperity, 100 years ago, as it celebrated its 700th anniversary. Like Ben Johnson's Cityscape it includes both existing buildings and others that were only planned at the time. The Liver Building was not completed until 1911. The Anglican Cathedral, on which construction started in 1904 and finished in 1978, is shown with the twin towers originally planned – the design was changed to a single tower in 1909–10. George's Dock appears where the Cunard Building now stands and the Manchester Dock lies where the new Museum of Liverpool is being built. A Cunard liner, possibly *Mauretania* or *Lusitania*, is moored at the Landing Stage, a remarkable structure first floated in 1847 that permitted millions of people to pass into and out of Liverpool. The city's overhead railway stretches along the dockland. Smoking chimneys punctuate the streets, their fumes cloaking the city. By contrast, this effect serves to spotlight the new Mersey Docks and Harbour Board headquarters (now the Port of Liverpool Building) and the Liver Building. Trams, a yellow Rolls Royce and women carrying parasols contribute to the scene's tremendous atmosphere. *Modern Liverpool* was shown during the Autumn Exhibition at the Walker Art Gallery in 1907 and prints of the view were available for purchase.

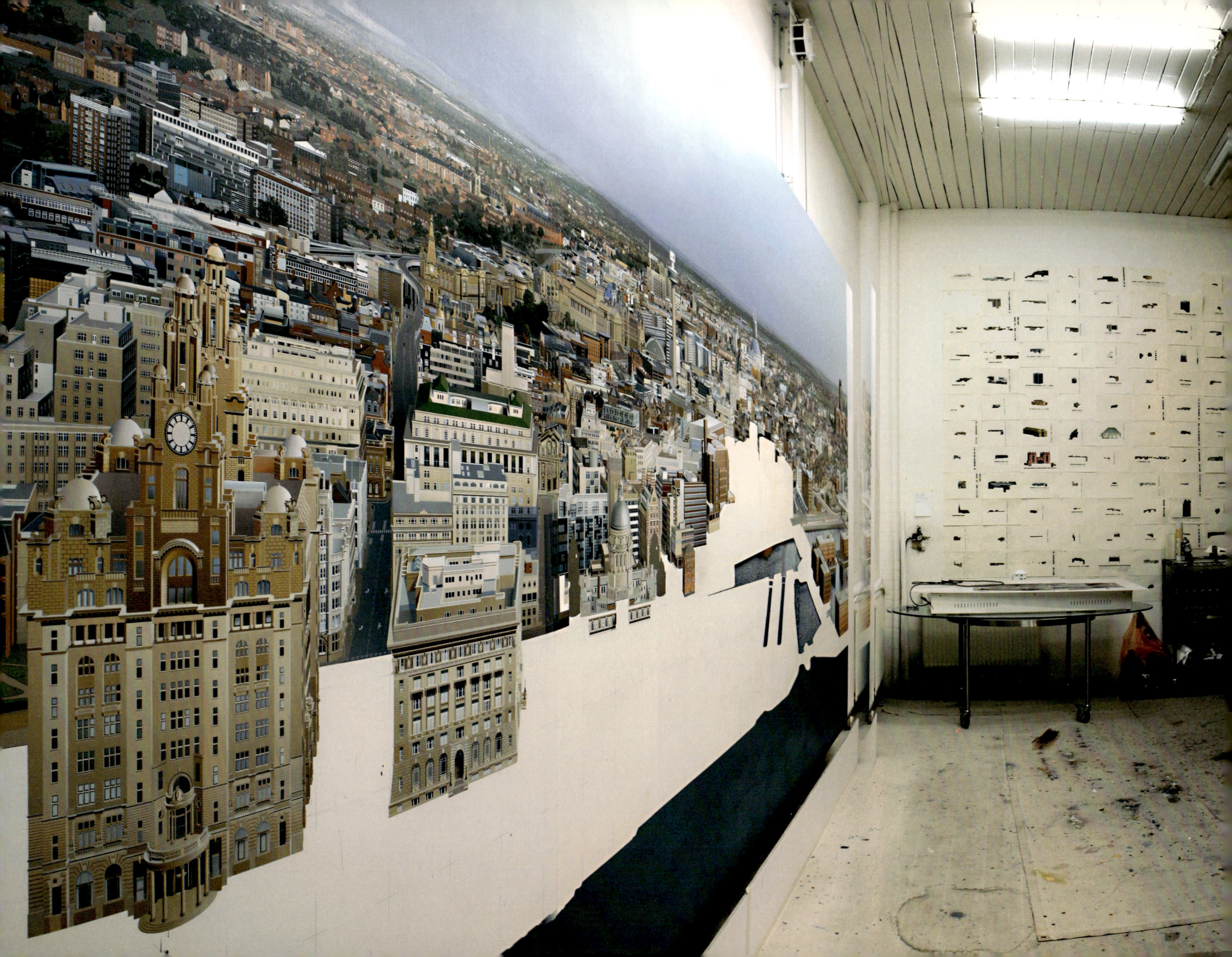

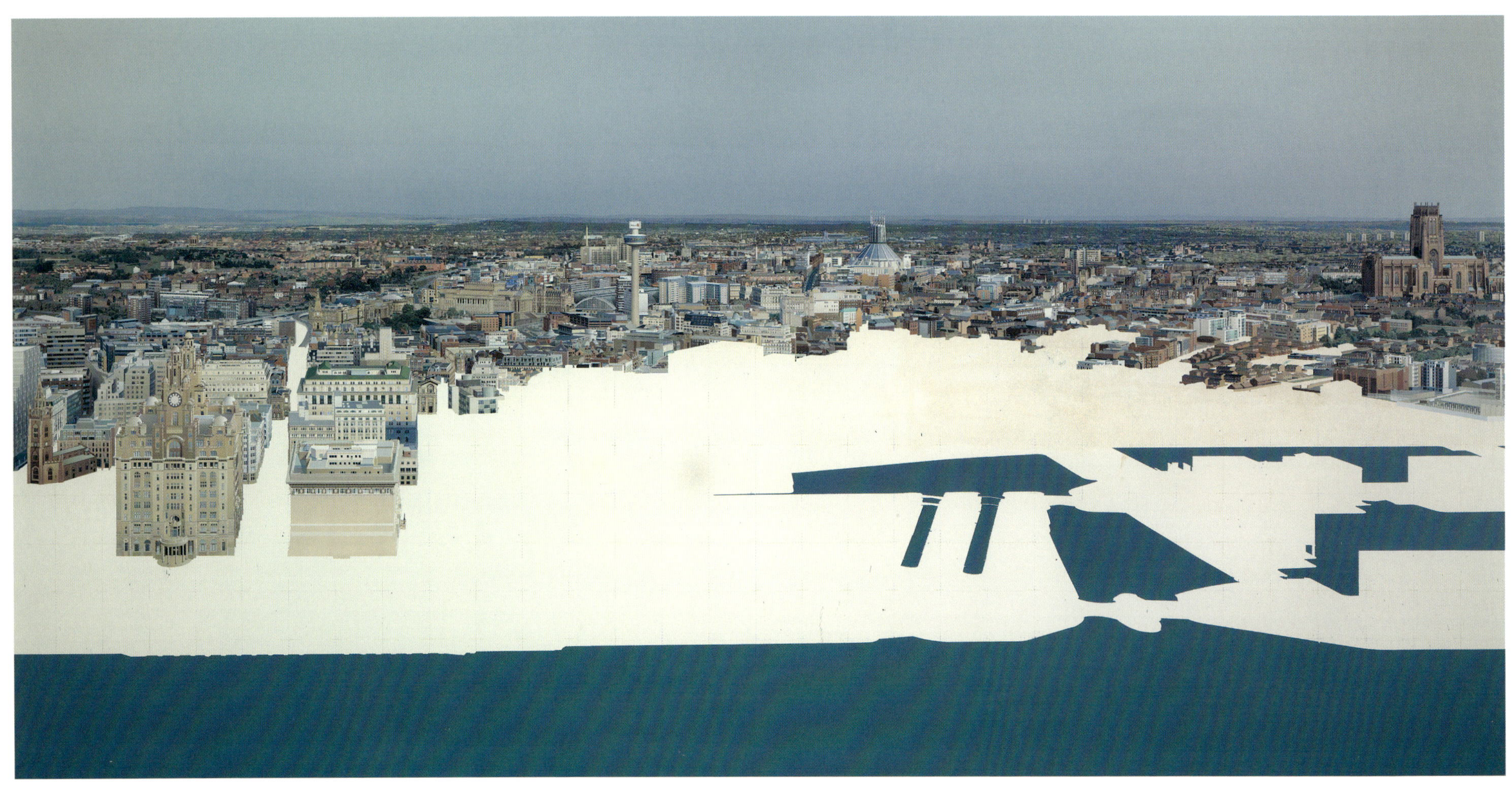

October 2007. Squaring-up of the canvas is evident on the unpainted areas.

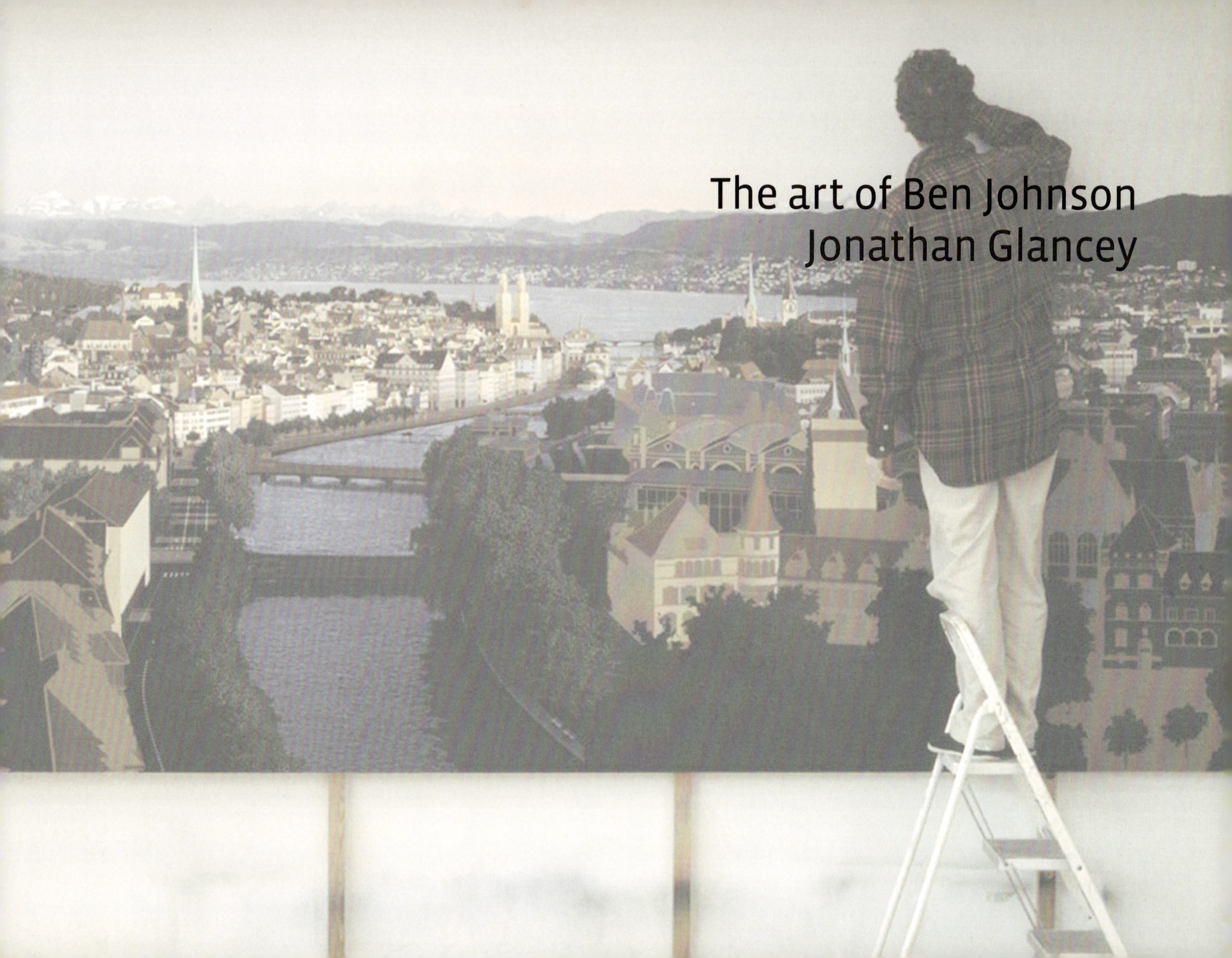
The art of Ben Johnson
Jonathan Glancey

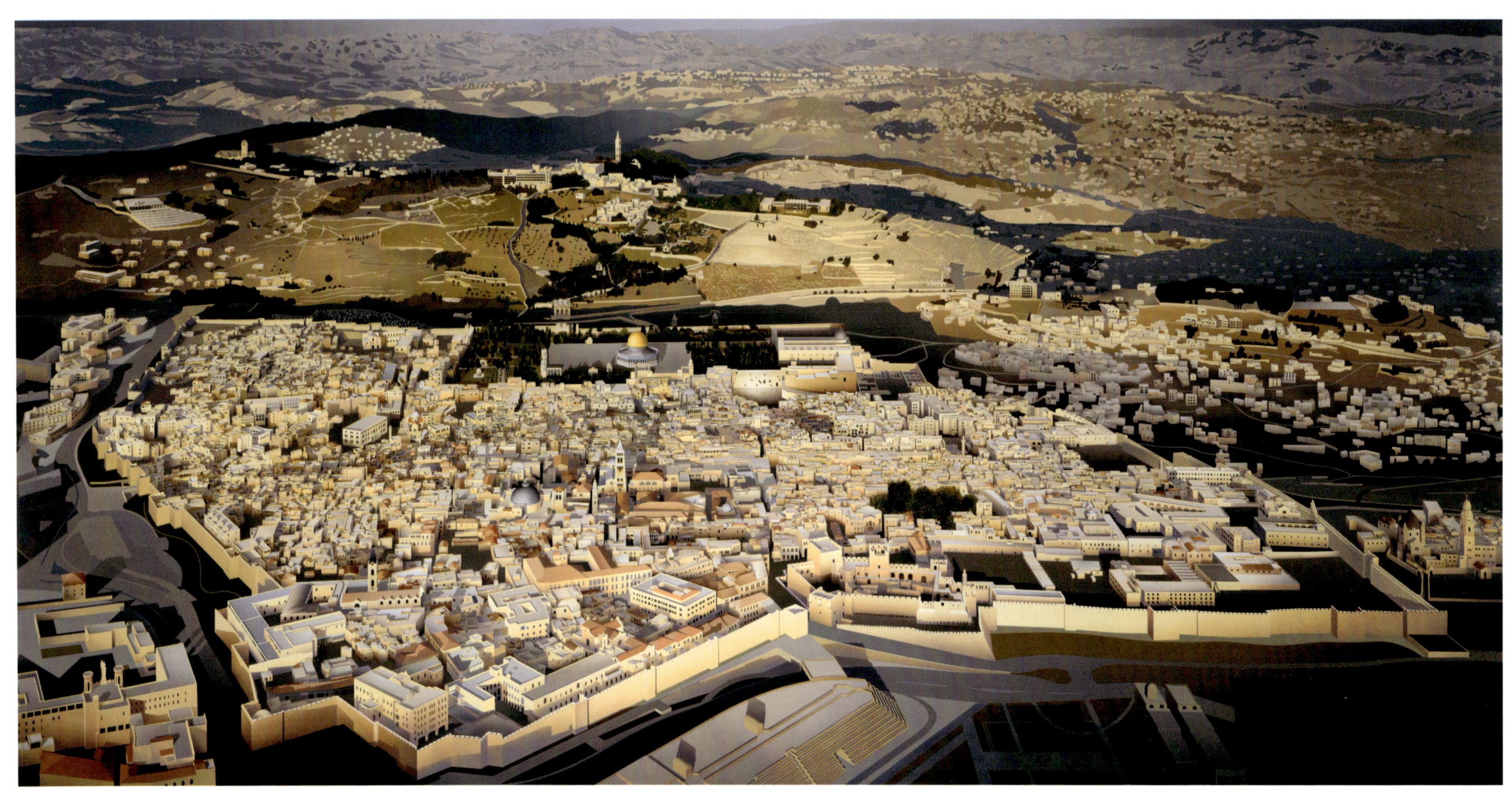

Jerusalem, The Eternal City, 2000
Acrylic on canvas: 229 x 457 cm
Reproduced by kind permission of the Khalili Family Trust, who commissioned the original work.

Ben Johnson was born in Llandudno. I haven't asked him this, and, in a way, I don't want to because it might spoil my illusion, or train of thought; but I can't help wondering whether, as a boy, he had ever taken the rope-hauled Edwardian tram up from the Welsh seaside town to the heights of Great Orme, one of the two ancient dragon head rocks that frame Llandudno and the sandy bay that fronts it. I ask this question because I came this way on a bright and still February morning when the sky was icy clear, the Irish Sea becalmed, and wheeling gulls muted. At this height, I could barely hear the sounds of the town below. No engines revving, no shouts of children sauntering to school, no dogs barking.

What I saw spread out beneath me on this freeze-framed morning was Llandudno looking more or less exactly like one of Johnson's city panoramas. Here, it seemed, were all the key elements that go to shape these extraordinary paintings: a distant – but not too distant – bird's-eye perspective of a town or city. A crystal-clear and unchanging light picking out each individual building as if it was under God's microscope. Utter stillness. And a sense that the town below me was a kind of abstract artwork, even though compressed, I couldn't help feeling, with all the riot of emotions expressed in Dylan Thomas's *Under Milk Wood*.

Johnson's panoramas, of Hong Kong, Jerusalem, Zürich and, now, Liverpool, all share this haunting, mesmeric sense of being somehow cool and detached and yet, at the same time, full of implied human activity and emotion. In Johnson's eye, though, this activity, and such emotion, are contained by his perfectly still representation of cities that we know to be bursting with energy.

What I think he might be saying is, 'Look, here is a city, recreated as a perfect image of itself; it's an unblemished, yet open book. It's here for you to populate it with your dreams, desires, and, perhaps, just yourself.'

Johnson's panoramas, then, might be perfect, acrylic simulacrums of real cities. They might, at first glance, seem all too chaste, with every scrap, rag and tag of life stripped from them. Yet at the same time they are invitations not just to look at familiar places from afar, but to engage with them as if we were seeing them for the very first time.

I was intrigued when, in 1993, Johnson recreated the famous Italian Renaissance image of the
town centre of Urbino. If the original of this dream cityscape appears to be so very coolly detached,
then Johnson's was, on one level, icily perfect. The artist entitled the painting *Footfalls Echo in the
Memory Down the Passage We Did Not Take Towards the Door We Never Opened*. The title is taken
from lines in the poem 'Burnt Norton', one of T. S. Eliot's *Four Quartets*. The thought Johnson clearly
wished to express is that of us, the viewer, standing perfectly still and looking into a perfectly
ordered world, perfectly created for us on canvas, one that we might just be able to inhabit, but,
of course, never can, because we are all too human, and no city could ever be so perfect once we
stepped into that immaculate Italian Renaissance piazza.

In this sense, Johnson's paintings are very human, the stuff, in fact, of a humanistic tradition in art
– as in architecture, city planning, and life – that shows us ideals of what might be; and because his
cityscapes are so intimately, beautifully rendered, Johnson offers us a chance to fall in love with the
cities we create with such hope and yet make a very human mess of day-to-day. I have heard it said,
many times, that Johnson's cities are like photographs. In fact they are nothing like photographs
at all. They are not images of reality, but of an imagined reality. Just look at the light that shines on
Johnson's cities and casts its refined shadows on their buildings and monuments. Here is a light that
does not exist in reality. It's a light that calls to mind other lines from Eliot's *Four Quartets*:

> Dust in the air suspended
> Marks a place where a story ended

In Johnson's cities, there is no dust. These cities appear to have told no stories. They are pure, as if
created at a click of some divine finger.

They are, almost if not quite, blank canvases upon which anything might happen. We, the observers,
can tell any story, or stories, we like. Each of us can populate Johnson's Hong Kong, or Liverpool, in
our particular way. Johnson has often painted corridors leading to doors – *Corridor of Contemplation*
(1990), *Reading Between the Lines* (1997), *Corridor of Benediction* (2000), *Passing Through* (2001),
Journey into Light (2001) – and whether these depict Italian Renaissance or ultra-modern English

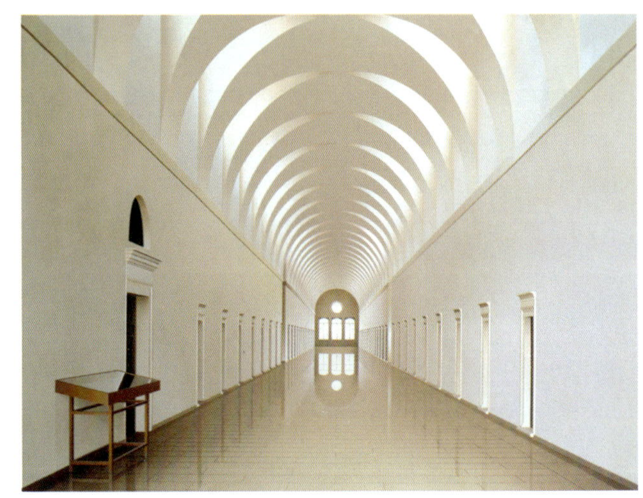

Corridor of Contemplation, 1990
Acrylic on canvas: 112 x 147 cm
Private collection

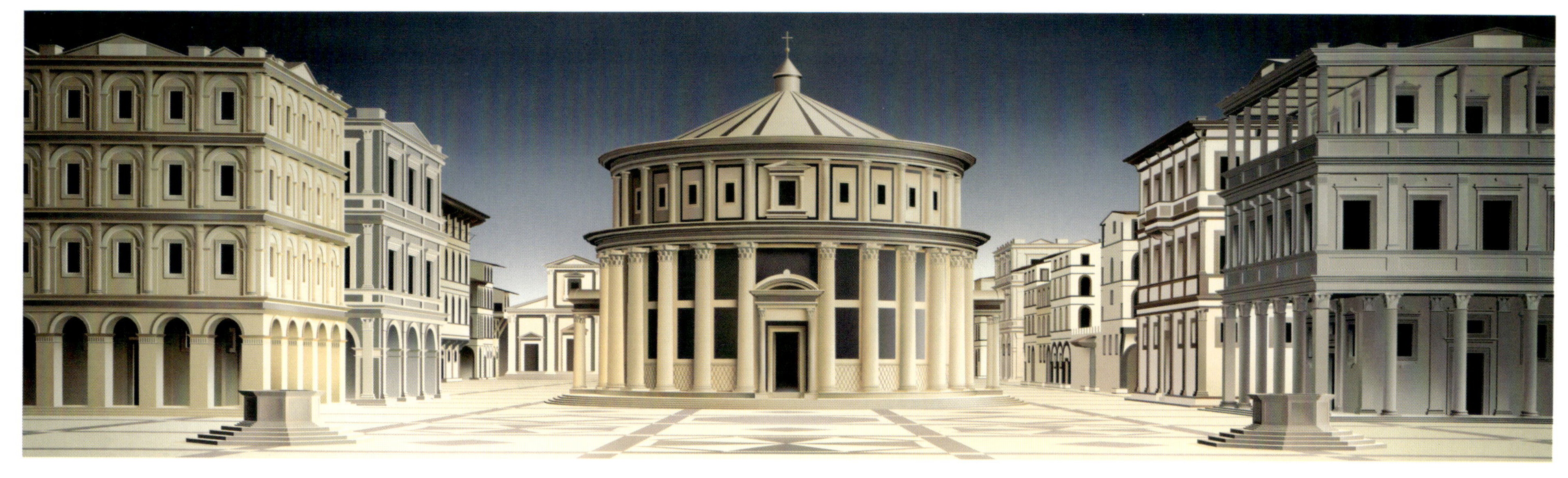

'Footfalls Echo in the Memory Down the Passage We Did Not Take Towards the Door We Never Opened'
Reconstruction of the Urbino Panel, 1993
Acrylic on canvas: 137 x 488 cm
Private collection

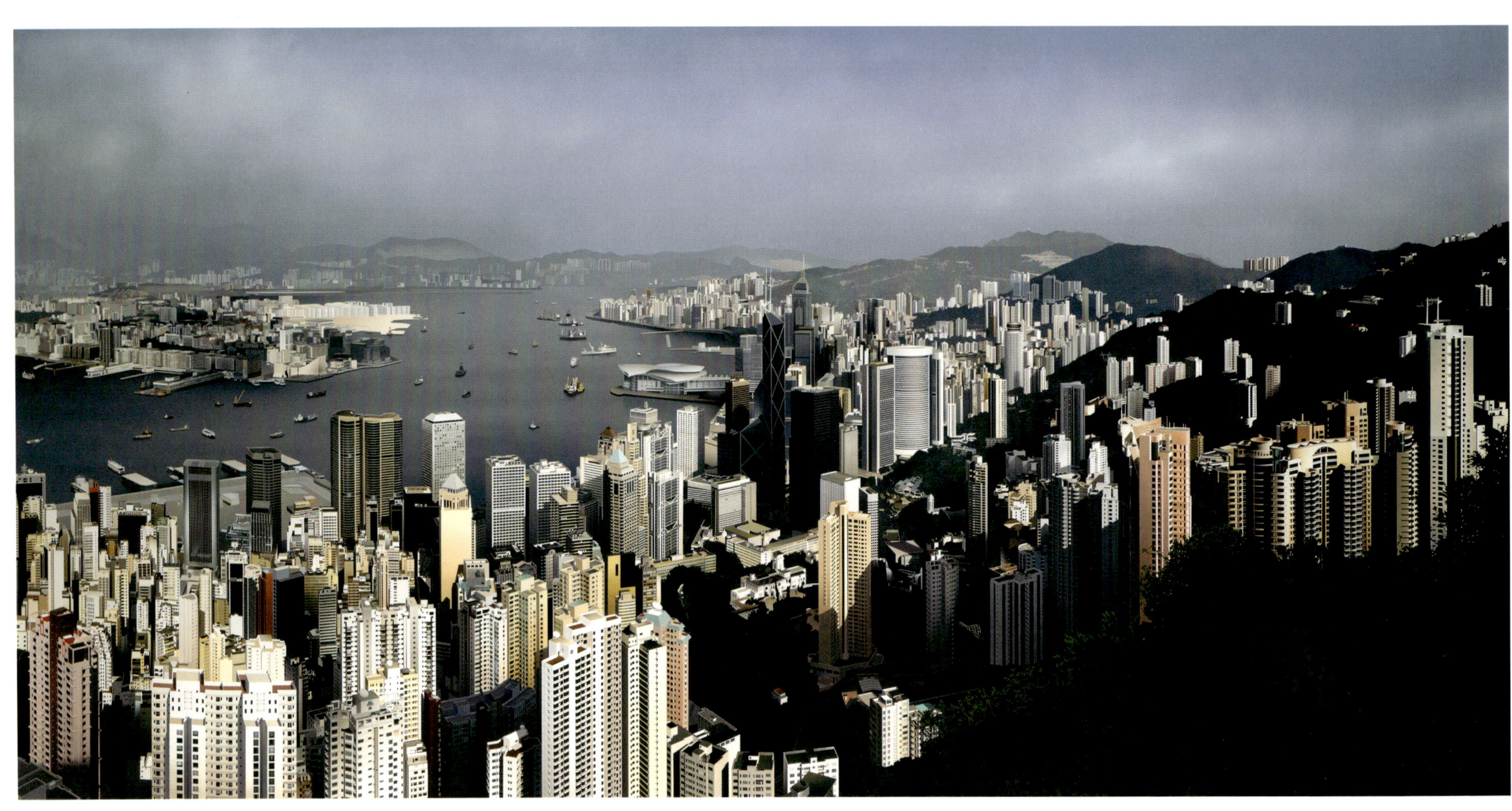

Hong Kong Panorama (Hong Kong, Energetic and Communicative), 1997
Acrylic on canvas: 183 x 366 cm

minimalist interiors, each presents us with a possible journey towards a door we might take, and so into a story of our own making, our own experience. Or, of course, we can stay outside the canvas, leave that corridor untrod, that door unopened . . .

So, Johnson's paintings play on our eye and psyche on several levels. On the one hand, they are seemingly perfect, still life, abstract representations of familiar cities; on the other, they are pregnant with possibilities. These are our cities. This, indeed, is what they look like, or seem to be, and yet we can make them anything we want them to be, if we are so minded. Liverpool, then, a city blessed with a superb architectural heritage, a romantic townscape, might yet be the great hub of culture it has claims to be in 2008. Johnson's panorama, seen from the perspective of a Liver Bird, allows us to see, and even to inhabit, in our imaginations a great seaport city free of the historic taint of the slave trade, or of industrial strife, or of troublesome '80s politicians, or urban decay and joblessness, and to imagine, as clearly as his eyes do, a city in excelsis. Just look at those wonderful buildings . . .

Mind you, Johnson's Liverpool cityscape also highlights the way that this city, along with most others in Britain, has been blighted over the decades, and continues to be blighted, by insensitive development and dismal new buildings. Johnson shows us a Liverpool to live up to. By stopping the city in its tracks and representing it as some apparently perfect object, Johnson allows us time, and thus the luxury of looking at it in a way that is at once detached and quietly emotional. The sense of deep calm he creates – not just here, but in all his paintings – helps us to imagine what might yet be. If you held this Liverpool in the palm of your hand, you would surely want to put it down again with its streets and squares, its parks and Pier Head inhabited by a content, as well as a lively people.

Johnson's city paintings, as he once told me, are on one level, 'An attempt to find that still point in the turning world T. S. Eliot searches for in the *Four Quartets*'. 'I hope that doesn't sound pretentious', he added, 'because I think it's something most of us search for in our more reflective moments. The paintings are about orientation and grounding, about a certain contentment you feel in an exact time under exact light.'

Leaving such thoughts aside, Johnson's panoramas are rightly popular creations because they are so very clearly works of immense and dedicated craft as well as beautiful and thought-provoking objects. I like the way Johnson is so very uninhibited in talking about the techniques he uses to create panoramas on such a vast scale. The site visits. The huge number of drawings made of cities and their individual buildings. The meetings with architects and planners that allow him to paint buildings that have yet to leave the computer screen for the construction site. The sheer computing power involved. Spray guns used to create lines just 0.2mm across. And, in the case of the Liverpool panorama, the use of 700 different colours, and so on into a litany of technical design and craft minutiae that is strangely compelling. Just as we gawp at the statistics – this amount of steel, that cubic footage of concrete – that goes into the shaping of some adventurous new bridge, so it's hard not to be excited by Johnson's technical wizardry. He is an artist happy to explain the secrets of his craft, and yet, of course, the end results of so much hard and technically involved work are paintings that are so very calm and serene that they seem effortless, and so perfect that it's hard to imagine them being shaped as much by an inventive use of design technology as by an imaginative eye, and a steady hand.

These ambitious paintings are monumental creations, and, like the buildings and cities they depict, they are the work of teams of assistants. Although seeking that 'still point in the turning world', Johnson's panoramas are very much about involvement and participation, by those who help shape them, to those who look at them, and, by extension, are invited by the artist to step inside them, to bring them alive in their own personal, and thus special, ways. *The Liverpool Cityscape* is a magnificent painting, as well as a kindly challenge to the Merseyside city. You can just about see Liverpool from the top of the Great Orme, by the way; and, with a very sharp and imaginative eye, perhaps all the world's great cities.

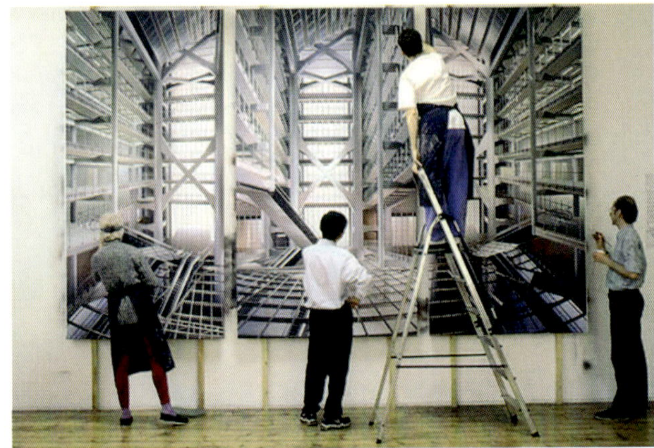

Three Moments of Illumination, 1998
Acrylic on canvas: triptych 274 x 432 cm

Ben Johnson at work on **Through Marble Halls**, 1994

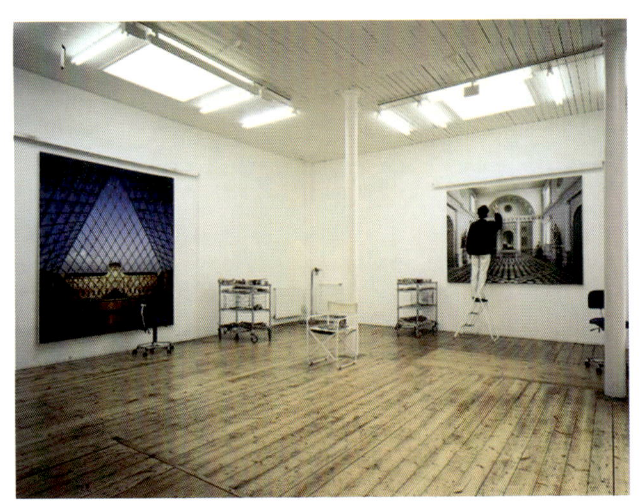

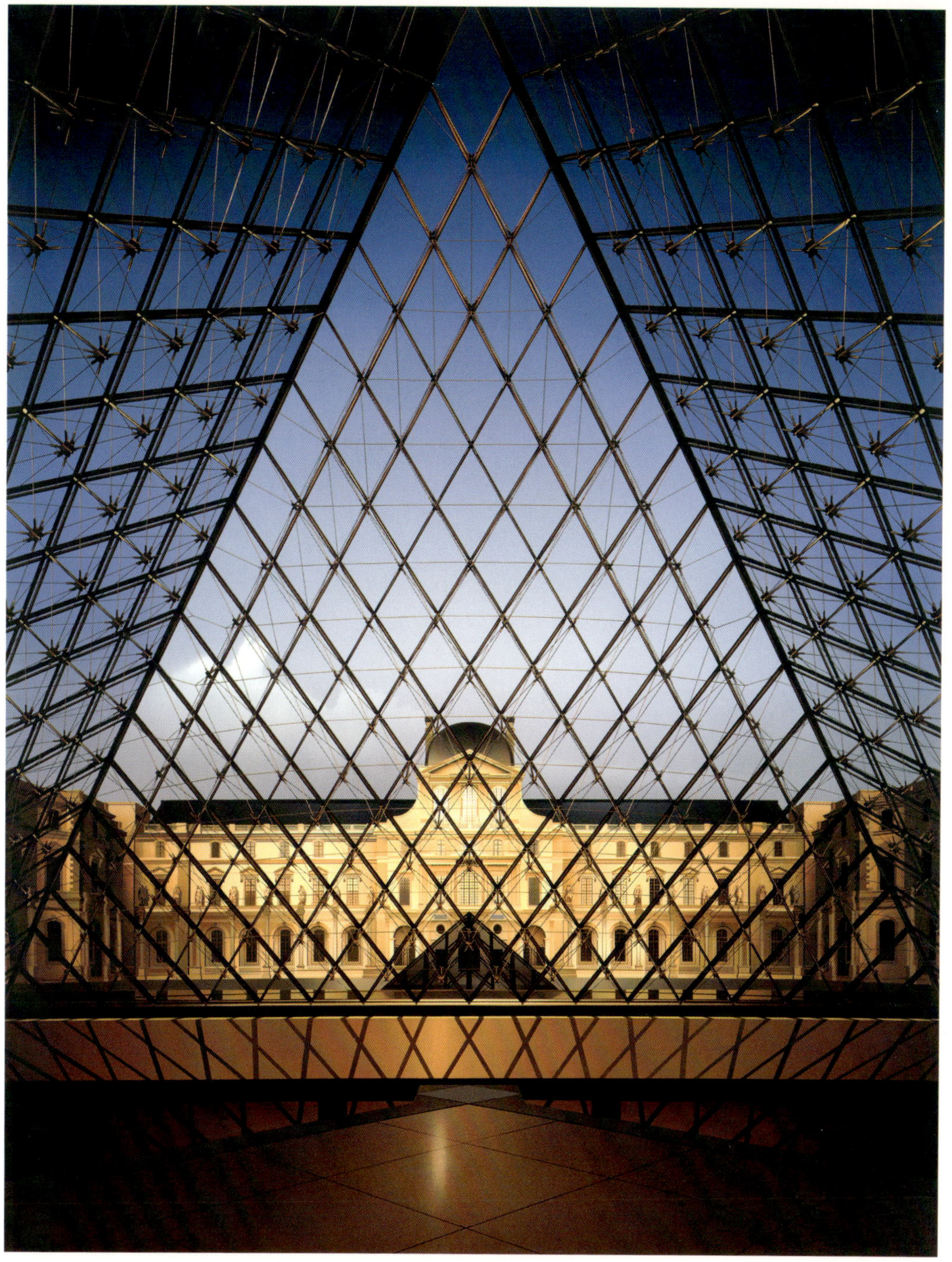

Reflections on Past & Present, Paris, 1996
Acrylic on canvas: 254 x 203 cm
Private collection

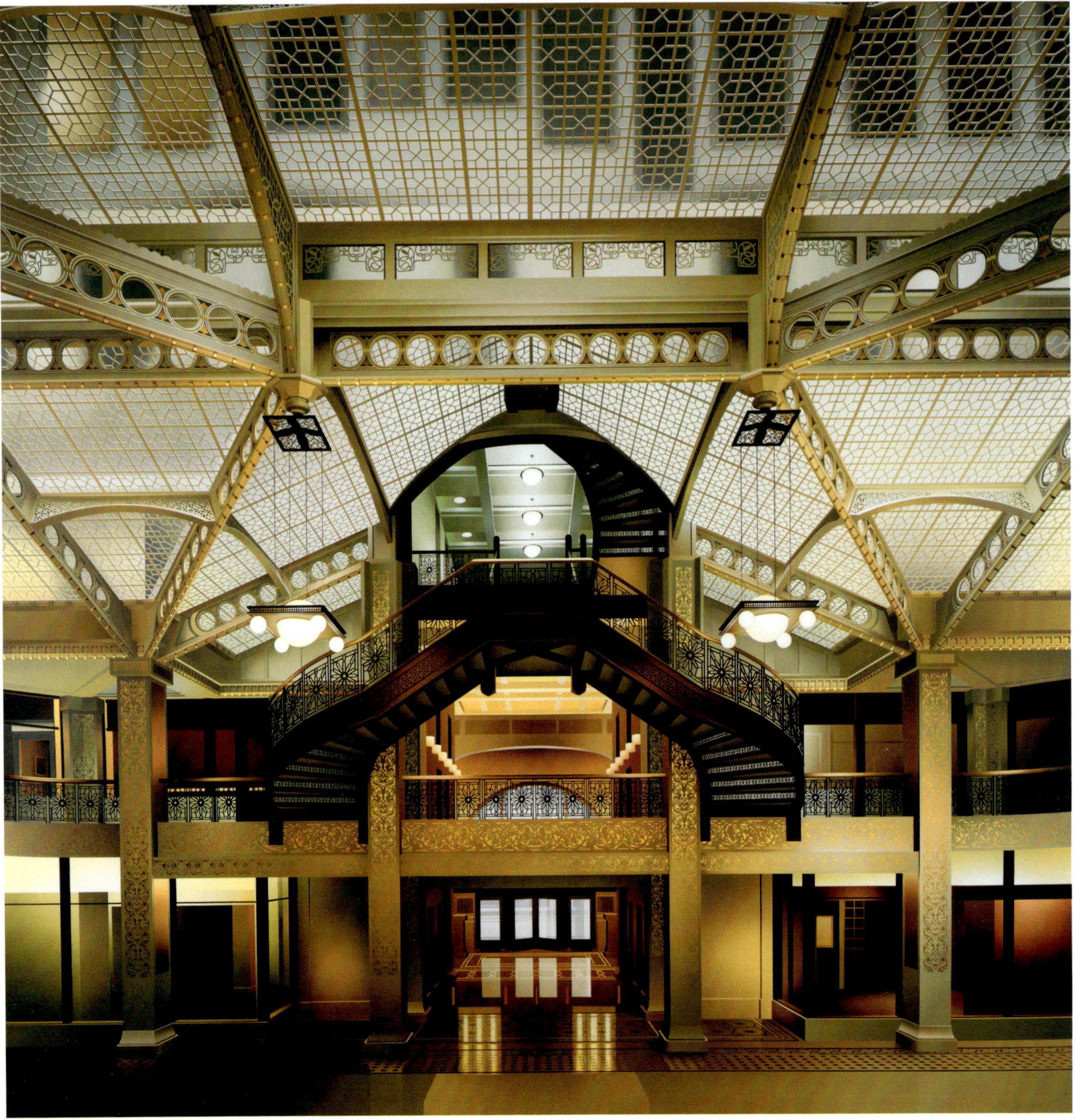

The Rookery, Chicago, 1995
Acrylic on canvas: 231 x 231 cm
Private collection

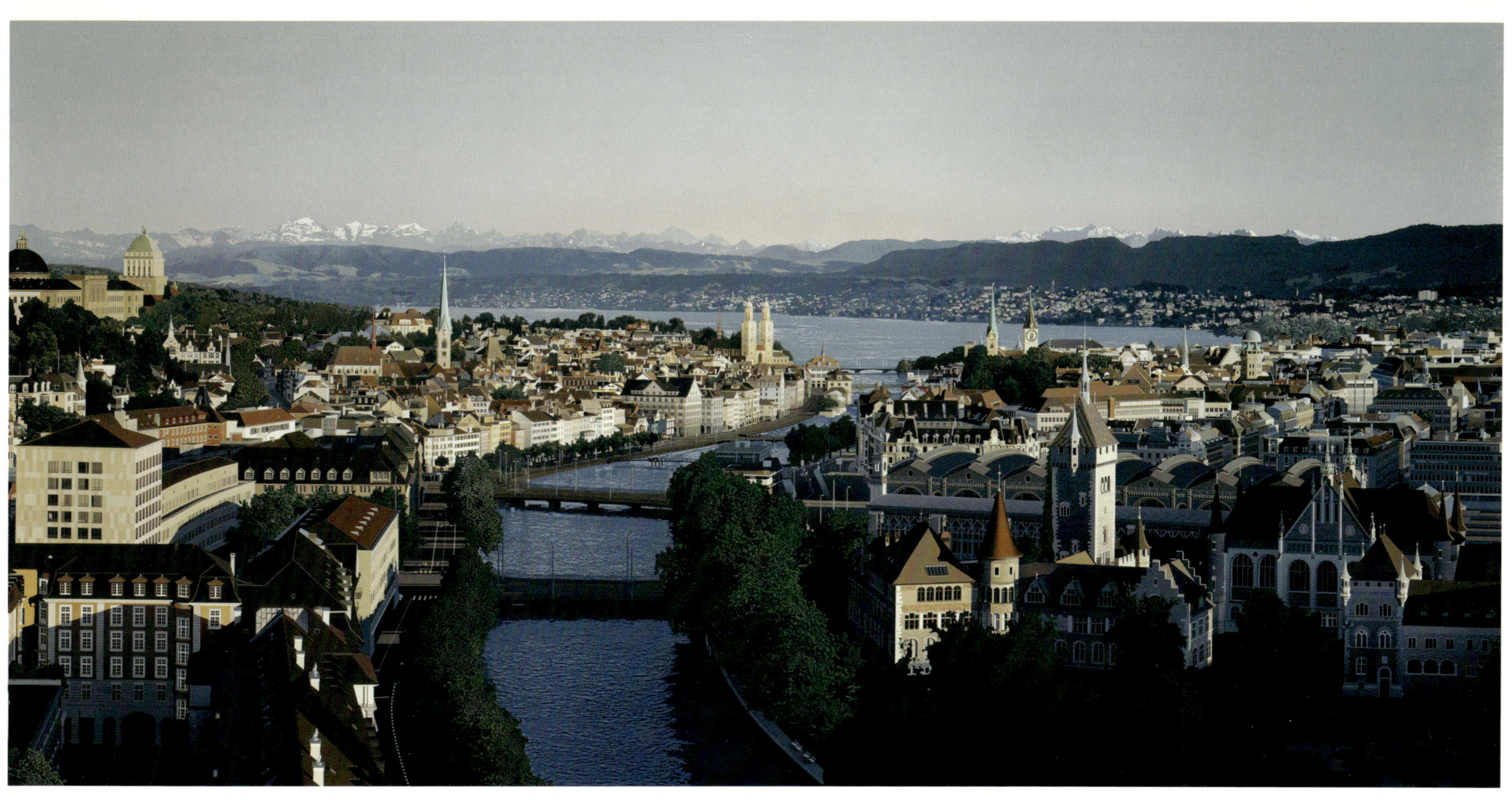

Zürich, 2003
Acrylic on linen: 200 x 400 cm
Private collection

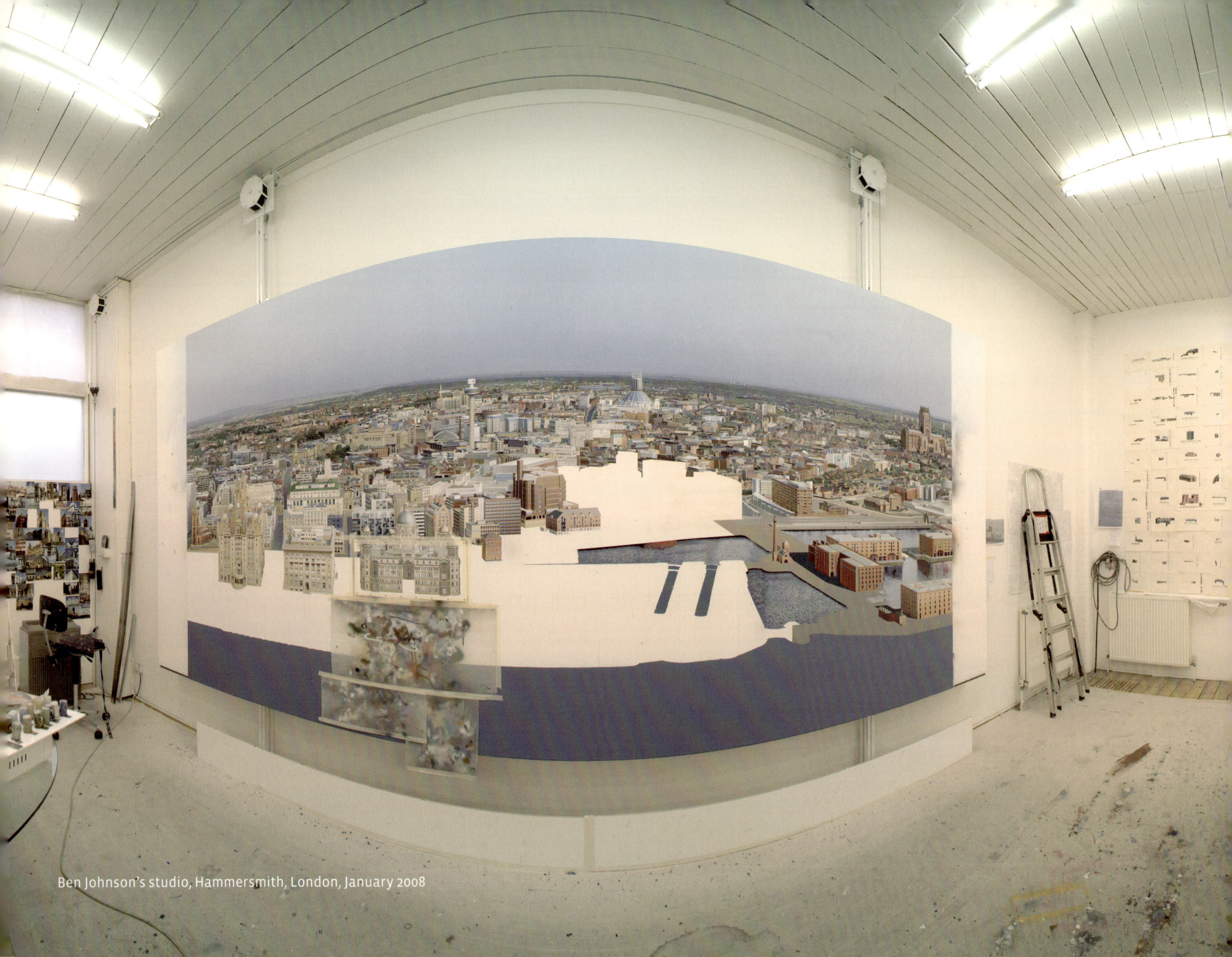

Ben Johnson's studio, Hammersmith, London, January 2008

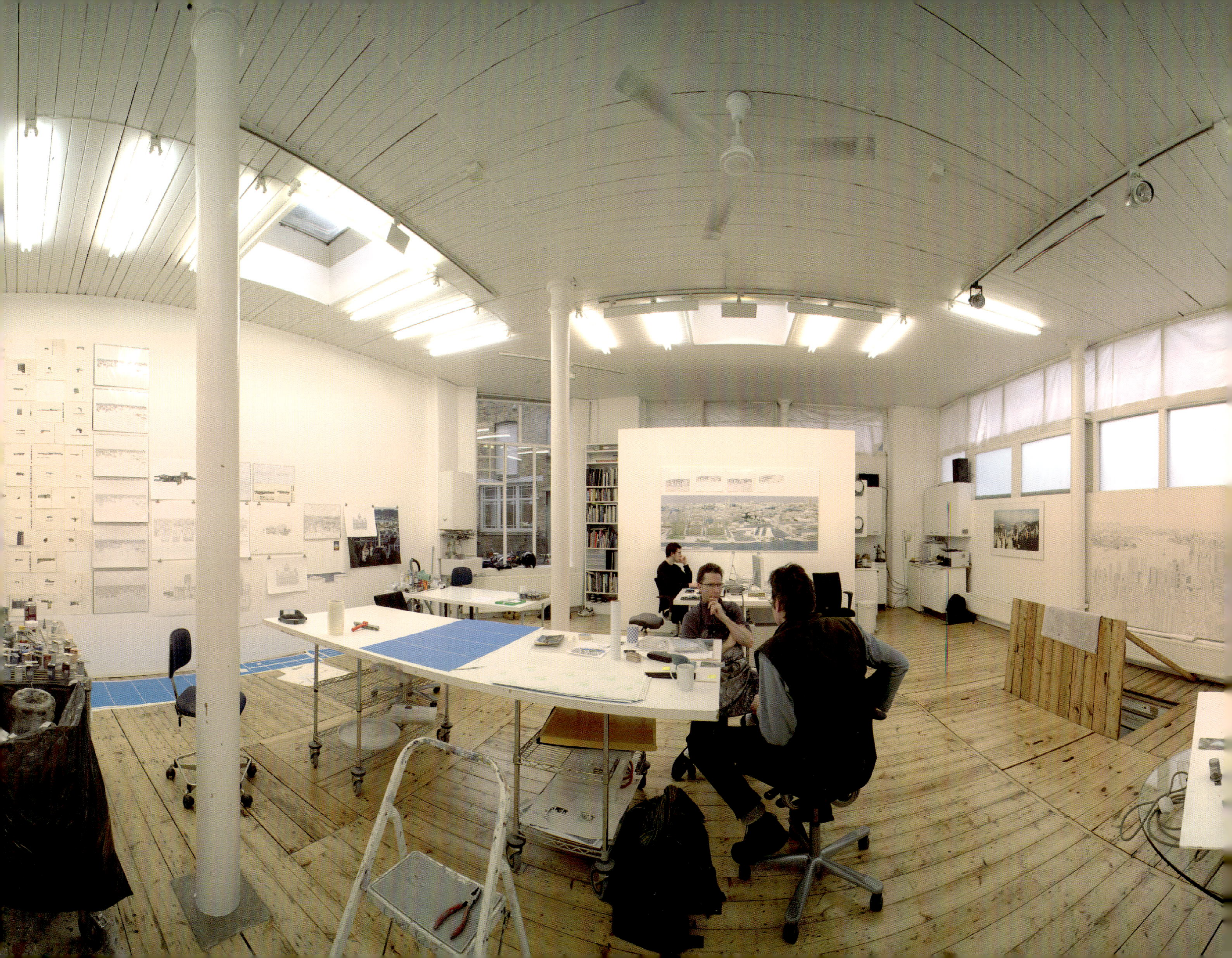

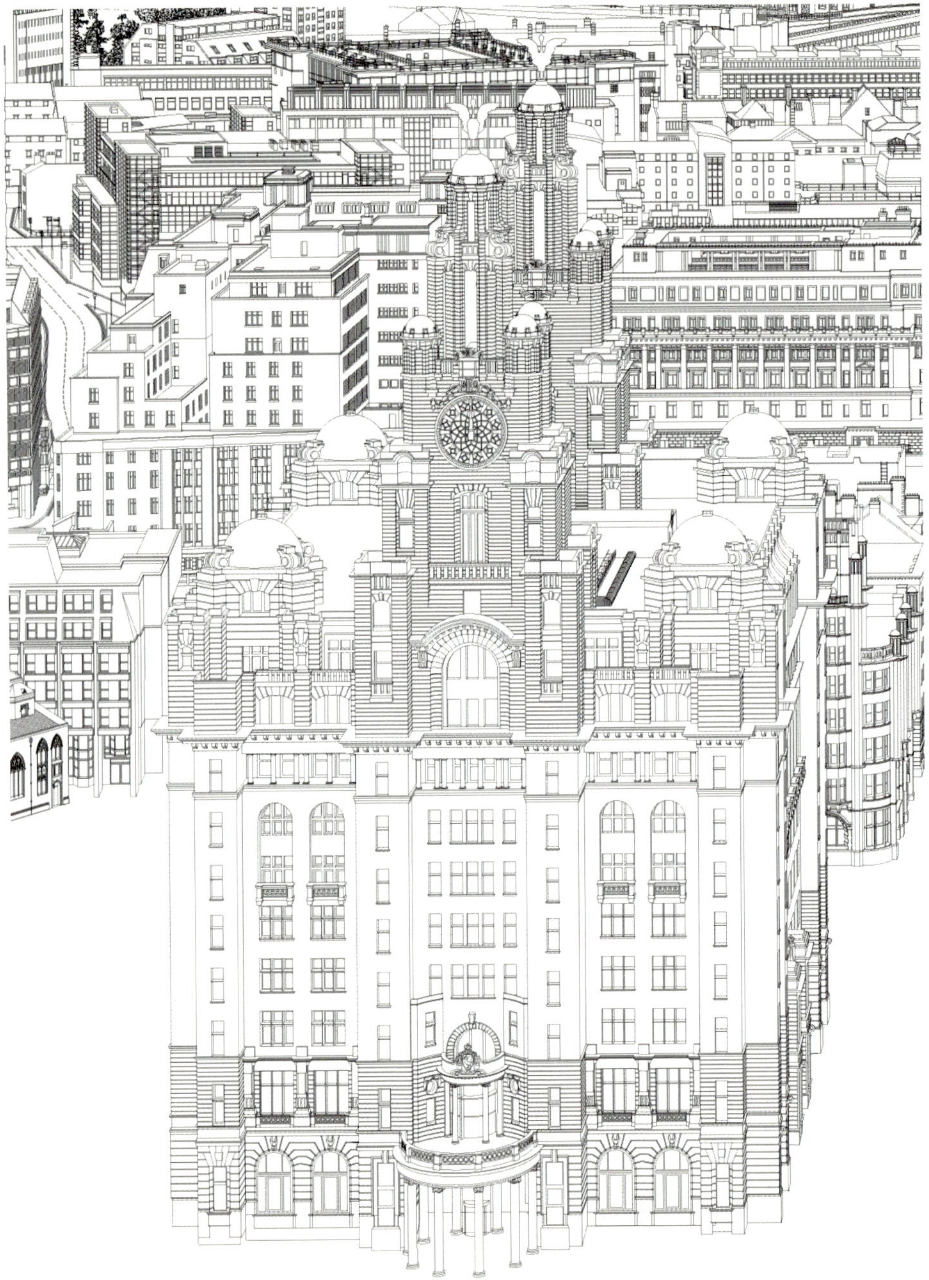

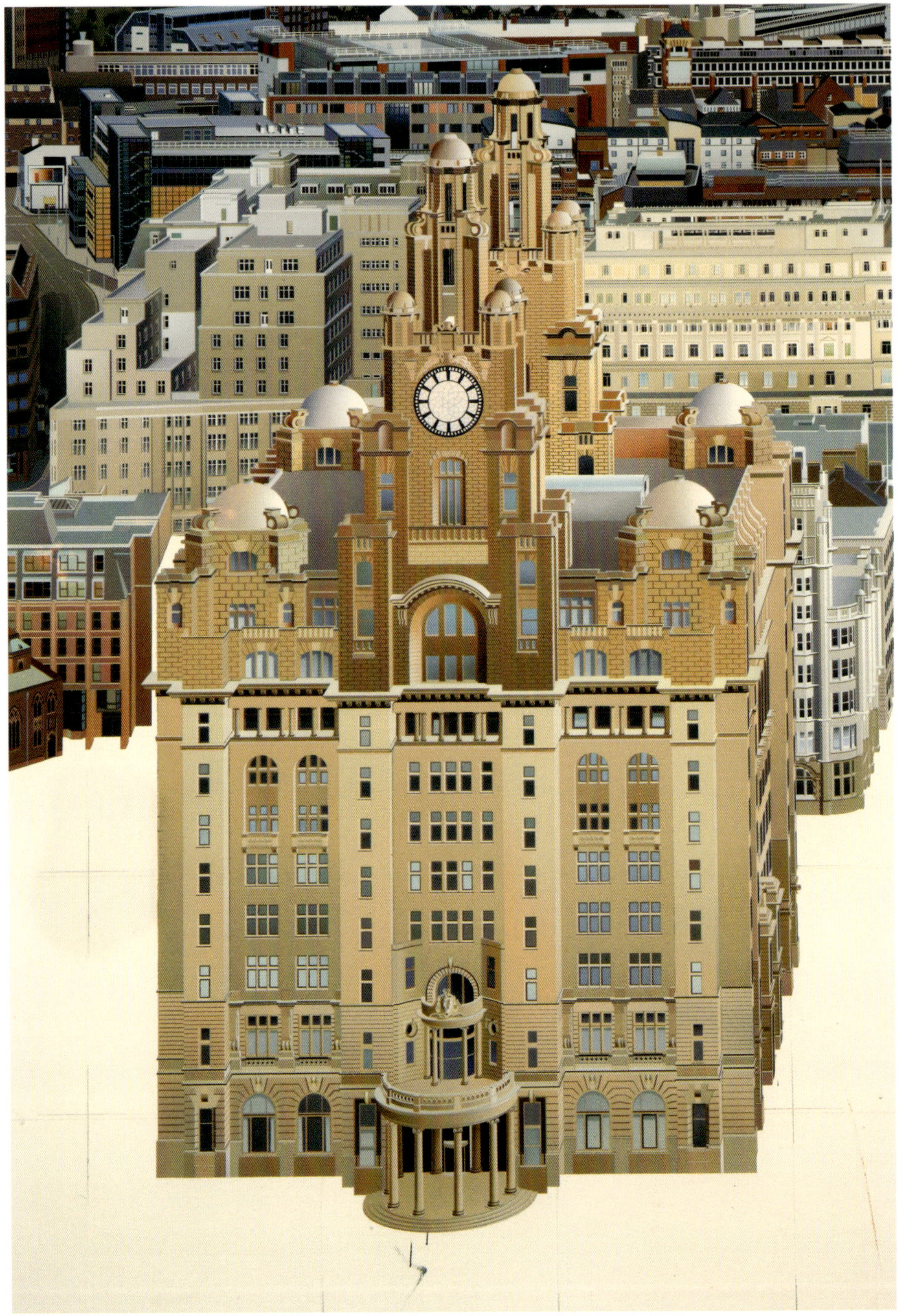

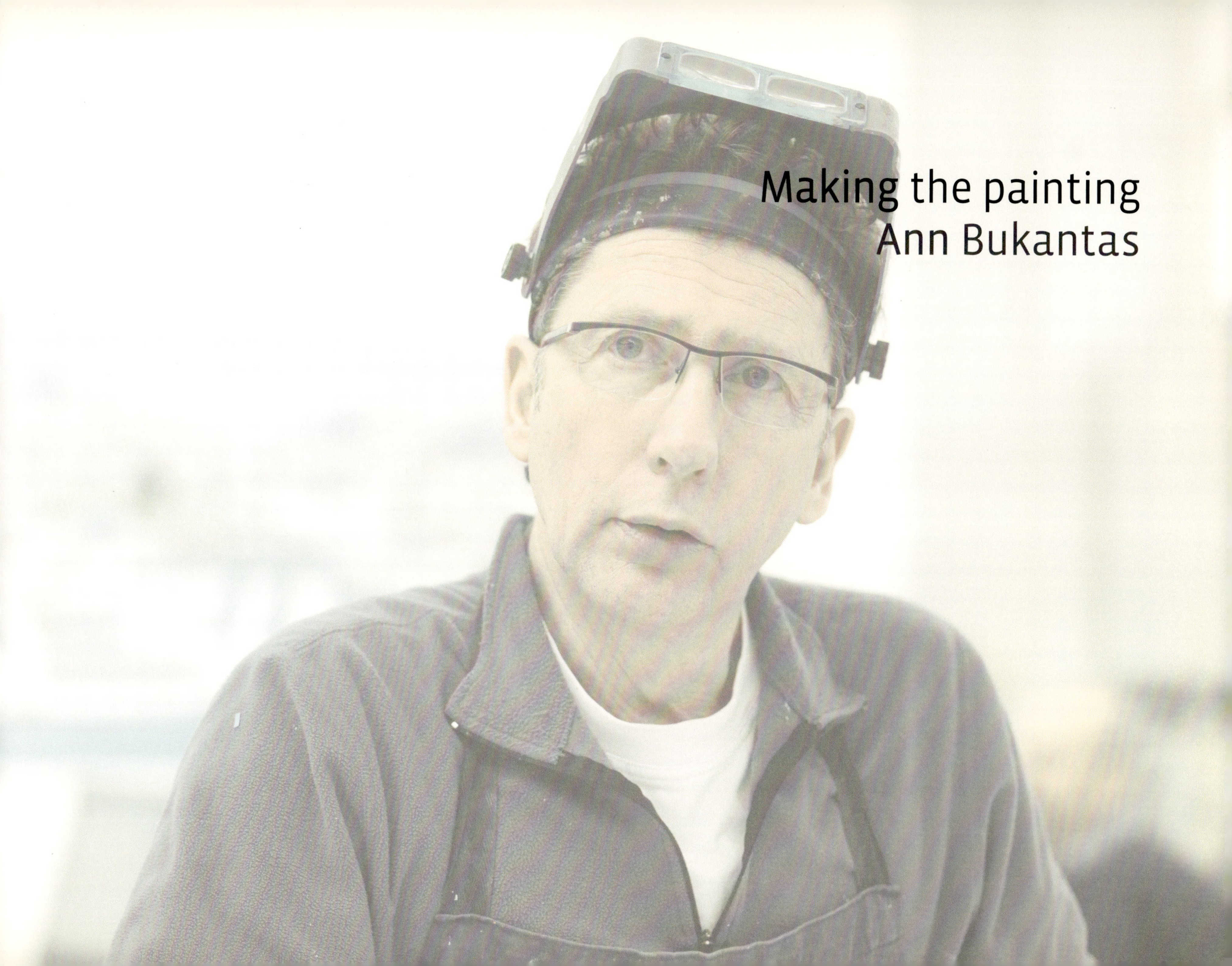

Making the painting
Ann Bukantas

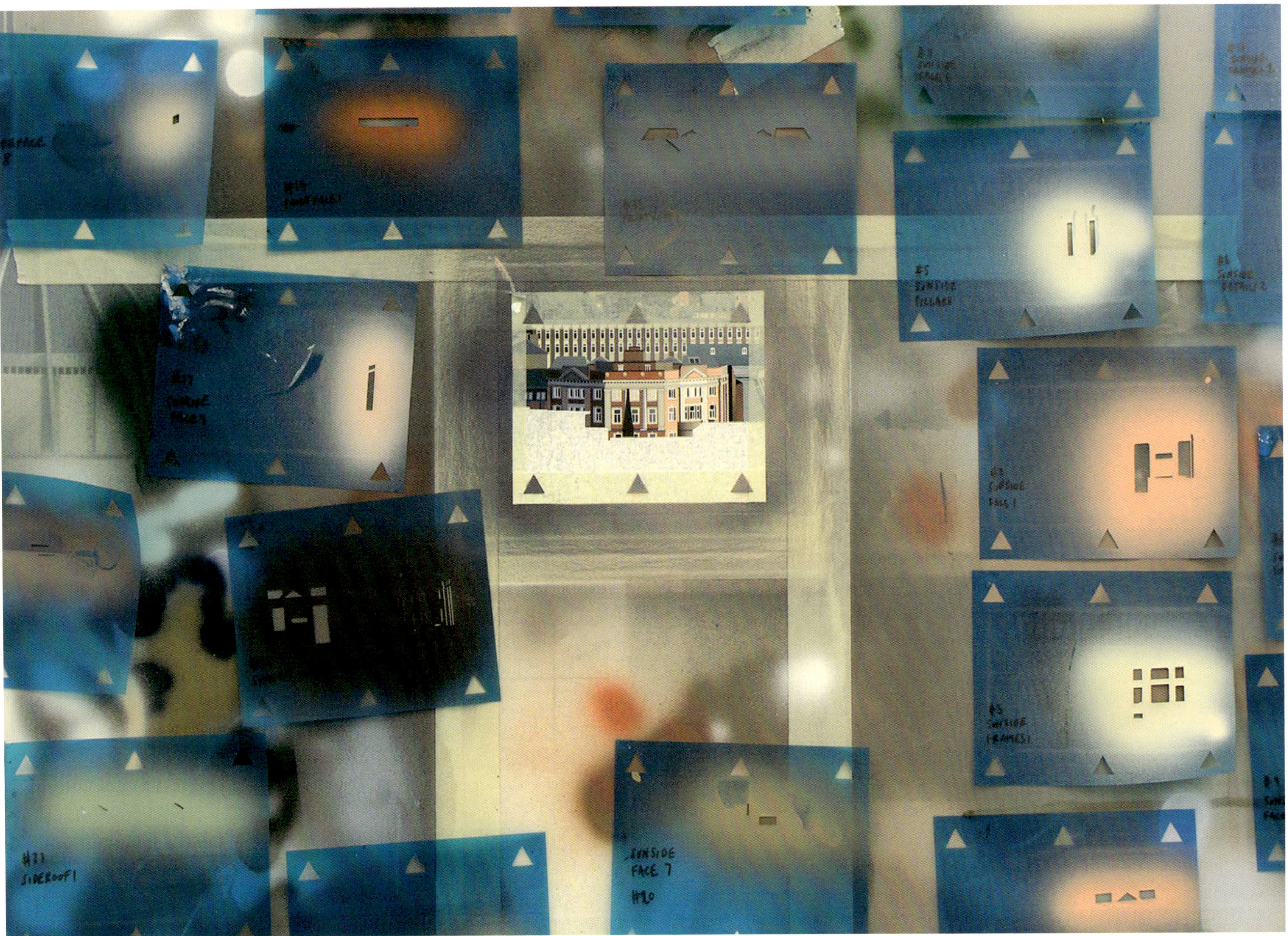

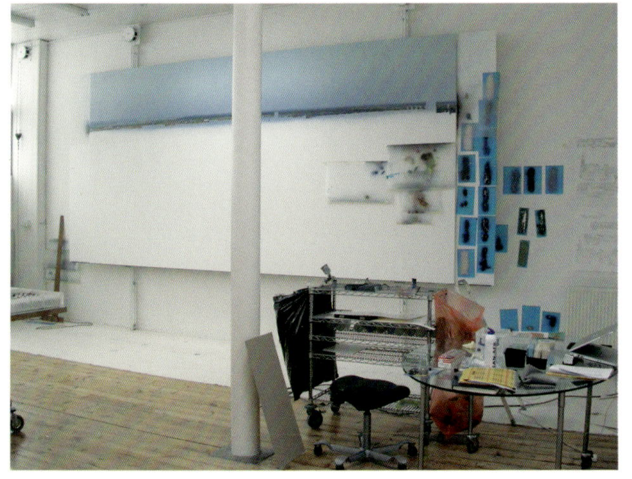

The Liverpool Cityscape is Ben Johnson's largest single-canvas painting to date and has been over three years in the making. He does not work alone on his city panoramas and Liverpool has been no exception. As one of the most ambitious visual records of a city undertaken, it is unsurprising that behind its production lies a complex but fascinating process and a group of talented, patient and steadfast people who share his awe-inspiring attention to detail.

Like his artistic predecessors centuries earlier, Johnson runs a busy studio – a team of individuals specialising in particular aspects of a painting's creation. Eleven assistants, with backgrounds ranging from fine art and illustration to painting conservation, have contributed to the Liverpool panorama. Their tasks have included computer modelling, colour mixing and stencil 'weeding'. Each effortlessly understands the others' role and operates in a way that is quite confounding to visitors yet is clearly an integral part of an industrious, productive and artistic whole. As 2008 dawned, the painting had occupied some 24,000 person hours.

The Liverpool Cityscape was commissioned from the artist in 2005. Johnson's track record in painting expansive detailed panoramas of cities including Jerusalem and Hong Kong made him an obvious choice to tackle such a well-known and well-loved subject at an important milestone in its history. It was perhaps inevitable that the chosen viewpoint was that for which the city is famous and one which has occupied artists and photographers for centuries. But the exact parameters were still tough to set. What would form the outer boundaries of the canvas at the left-hand (north-east) and right-hand (southern) edges? What buildings could not be left out and which would be prominent? How far back would the detail extend? Months of research and photography went into this early planning stage. The final viewpoint was agreed by the artist in discussion with representatives from the Cityscape's commissioners.

Liverpool's celebrated skyline is presented from a vantage point high above the River Mersey, 220 metres above sea level (at a point just above the Royal Liver Building's Liver Birds). The overall view comprises some eight square kilometres of the city, taking a raking bird's-eye view rather than an overhead aerial perspective. From a position 500 metres out into the Mersey from the iconic 'Three

Graces', the eye is led in a direct line up Water Street into the city's suburbs and the landscape beyond. Johnson presents the city in the context of its historic Lancashire setting.

The painting encompasses several thousand individual buildings and employs a subtle distortion of perspective and geography to combine some of the city's key features. The Greek Orthodox church, for example, has been moved inwards and upwards, its domed towers appearing to the right of the Anglican Cathedral. The Chinese Arch has also been elevated. The Everton and Liverpool football grounds have been brought closer together so that both are included in the upper left section, just below the horizon. Overhead, the sky is a crisp, clear blue that typifies the skies Ben saw on his visits.

Masts, wires, scaffolding and litter are all excised. Such artistic licence is extended to the lighting on the scene. The sun has several positions and there is consequently an ambiguous time of day, contributing to the eerie stillness that bathes the city.

Research

Johnson commenced work on the Cityscape in 2005, during Liverpool's construction boom in the run up to Capital of Culture year, 2008. This was both a challenge and a motivating force that drove him to capture the commercial and physical effects of its forthcoming European cultural status.

A commitment was made to include any new buildings that had clear architectural plans and confirmed planning permission, and which would definitely be built, even if they were not to be completed by 2008. To achieve this Johnson liaised closely with the planners, developers and architects who were working on the city, ensuring his vision was as contemporary as possible.

During his early research trips to Liverpool Johnson also met with experts in the history and architecture of the city, making a network of contacts who advised him as the project progressed. Access to some of the area's tallest structures was also vital in securing the photographic reference images needed. He was escorted nervously to the rooftops of some of the city's most iconic buildings. Among those he ascended were St John's Beacon, the Royal Liver Building, the Anglican

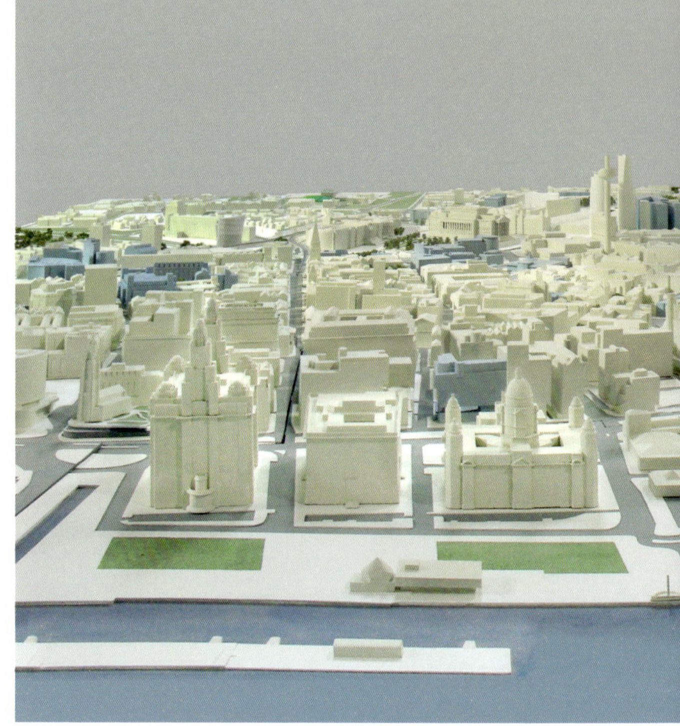

The three-dimensional model of Liverpool city centre

Photographic collage for proposed Cityscape viewpoint

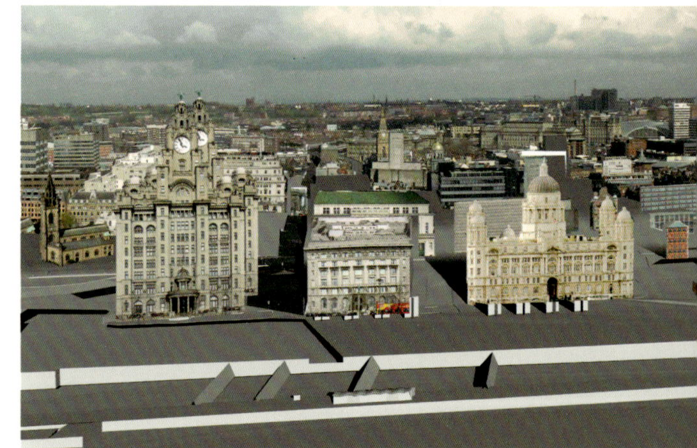

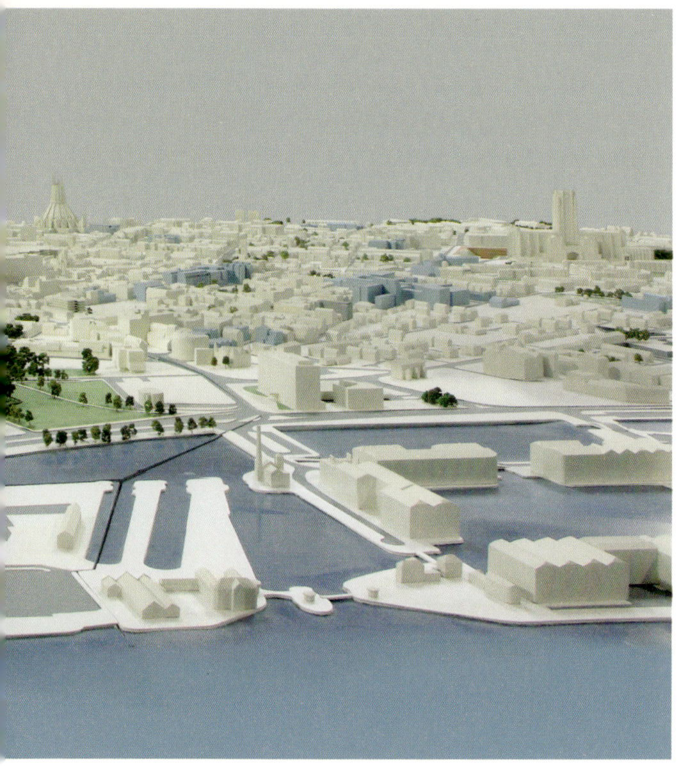

Cathedral and the Mersey Tunnel ventilation towers on both sides of the river. The Liver Building and Cathedral were essential positions from which to acquire an understanding of the city's layout.

Equally critical to the preliminary phase was a remarkable three-dimensional scale model of Liverpool city centre, originally constructed between 1961 and 1994 for the council's Planning Department. At five by four metres and built at a scale of 1:500, the model covers five square kilometres of the city. This model was photographed thoroughly from every angle by Johnson and his assistant Richard Gibson during 2005 in Liverpool's Static models studio and gallery space, where it was installed for repair and updating. There was no one spot from which to take an overall photograph of the city, therefore the model was instrumental at the outset in establishing the viewpoint for the Cityscape. Photographs of individual buildings and street blocks within the model would also subsequently be used to fix the correct perspective of their equivalents in the painting.

Indeed, photographs form a vital part of Johnson's research and source material. In repeated visits to Liverpool, usually chasing particular lighting conditions in which the surface colours of buildings were heightened, he took over 3,000 reference photographs. Countless buildings, streets and vistas were recorded from a variety of directions and rigorously logged back in the studio. These visits were also an opportunity for him to absorb the unique atmosphere of the city and to speak to local people, informing his final approach.

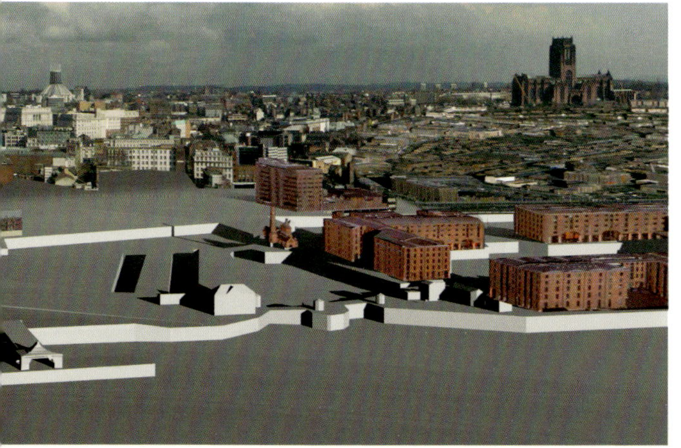

The painting itself

Ben Johnson abandoned his paintbrush years ago in favour of a spray gun to hide the stylistic 'signature' that is inseparable from an artist's brushstrokes. He similarly stopped painting people – noticeably absent from his cityscapes – feeling he was not humble or skilful enough to capture the human figure. *The Liverpool Cityscape* is therefore created, almost in its entirety, using a spray gun loaded with acrylic paints. Every inch of the painting is considered as important as the next. The wider image grows from a series of intricate, closely observed miniatures that combine to form the whole, sprawling panorama.

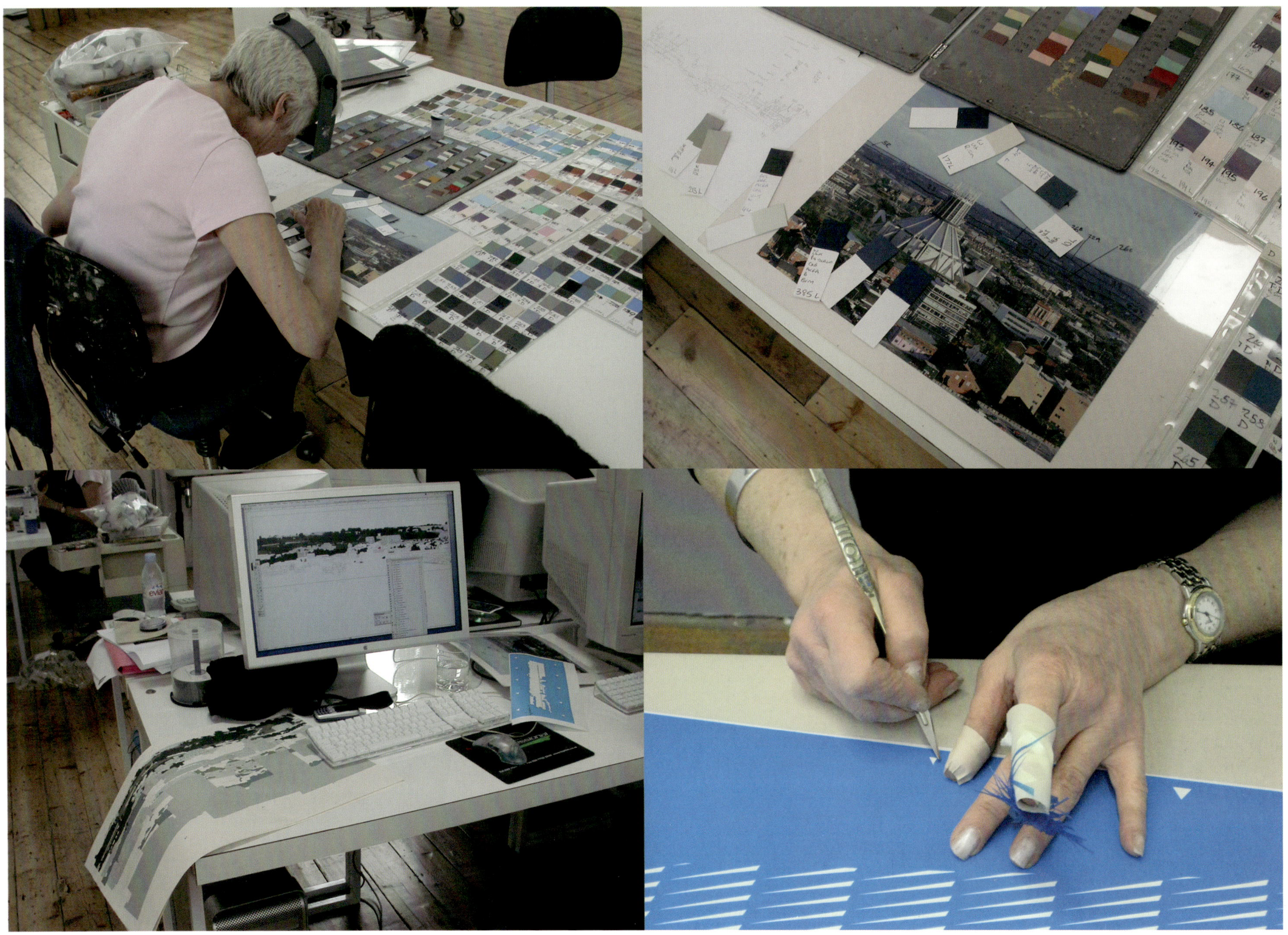

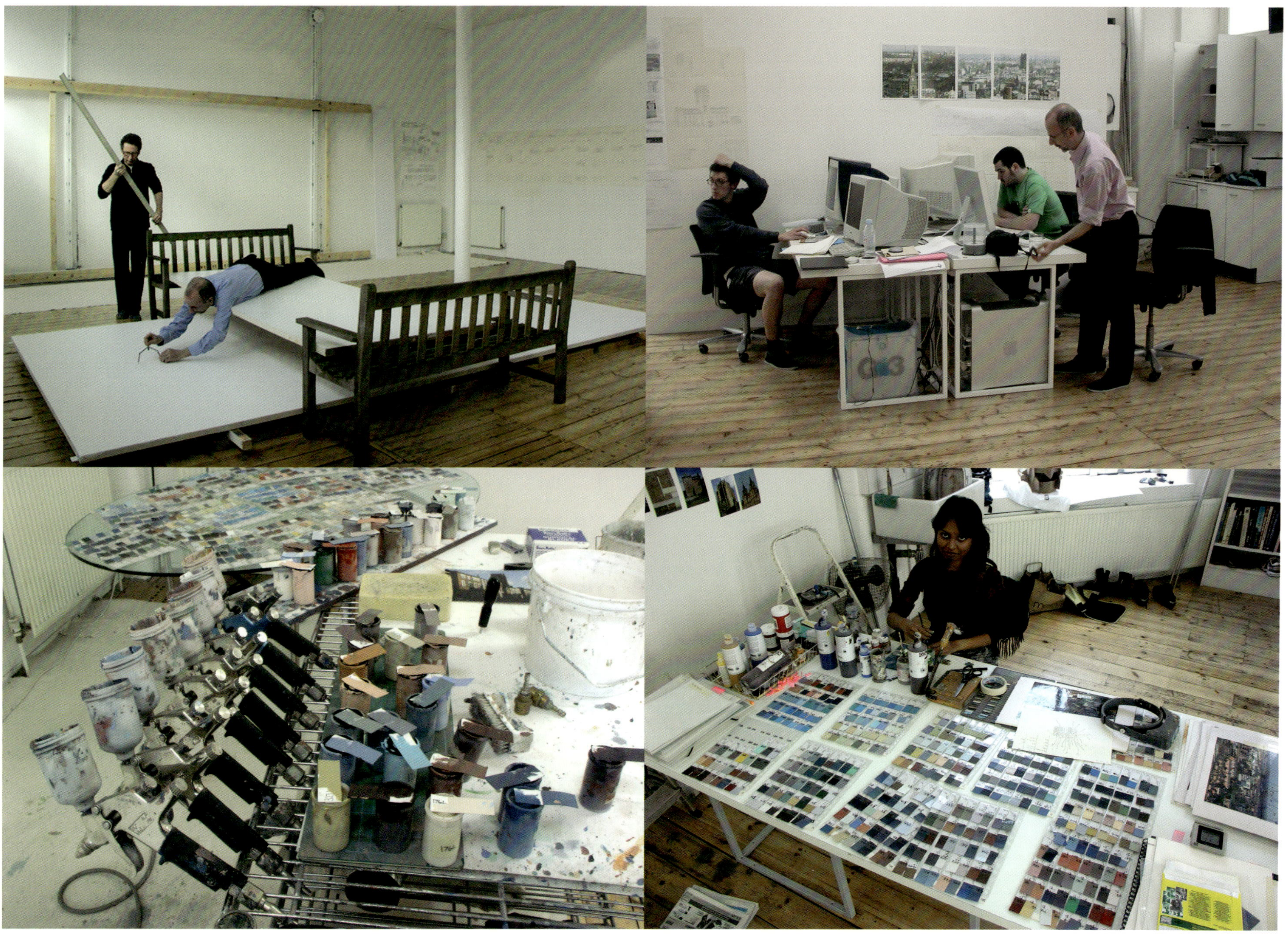

The size of the painting, at 244 by 488 cm (eight feet by sixteen feet), demanded rigorous construction methods. A large, cross-barred pinewood stretcher to hold and support the cotton duck canvas was made by the specialist firm Bird & Davis. A 'gator foam' board and polythene were placed behind the canvas for additional support and to act as a vapour barrier. A hoist was constructed in the artist's west London studio to raise and lower the canvas, making working across its surface less of a challenge.

The canvas was primed on both sides with multiple coats of acrylic gesso (a smooth, white preparatory layer) and a final coat of bright titanium white added. Over this foundation the canvas was marked up with a pencil grid of six-inch squares, enabling the Cityscape's outline to be accurately plotted using Ordnance Survey maps and a collage of computer-generated drawings. Then, starting with the sky, Johnson commenced work, from the top of the canvas downwards in a succession of horizontal bands. The background landscape came next. Towards the centre, as the buildings became more clearly defined, he worked across from left to right.

Johnson's preparation for painting a building or set of buildings is a lengthy, complex process. A series of vinyl stencils, through which the paint will be sprayed, must be created. Once the area of the city has been selected and relevant photographs assembled, a detailed line drawing is made on a computer using a vector-based (geometric modelling) programme. Johnson's team uses Adobe Illustrator. Each line drawing can take from a few days up to two months to prepare. The drawing's perspective is determined by overlaying it onto a photographic image of the city model. The drawing is then separated into various sections depending on its construction, colour and tone. From these, separate cutting files are created and sent through to a cutter to generate stencils for the specific part of a building or landscape feature – the brickwork, the window frames, shadows beneath the window frames, panes of glass, the foliage of a tree, and so on.

Previously, masking tape was used to create the stencils, a laborious and intricate task using scalpels to cut countless strips of tape, some as fine as three millimetres. The employment of the computer-driven cutter, normally used in the sign-writing industry, has superseded the manual approach,

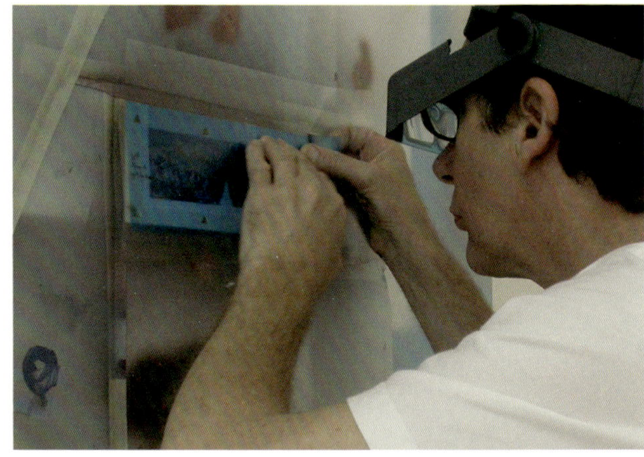

Clockwise from above: applying a stencil to the canvas; spraying the paint; drying the paint; removing stencil vinyl

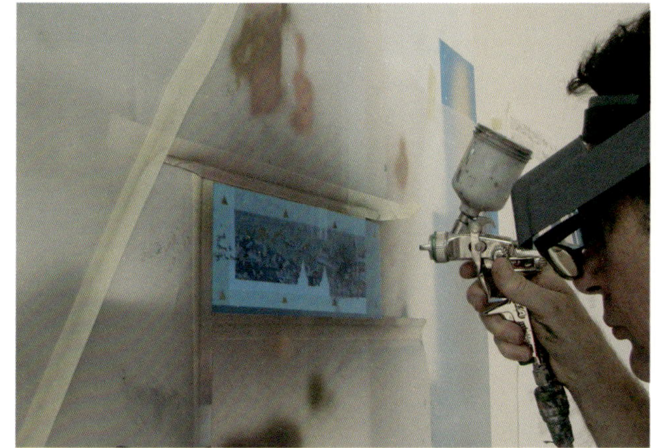

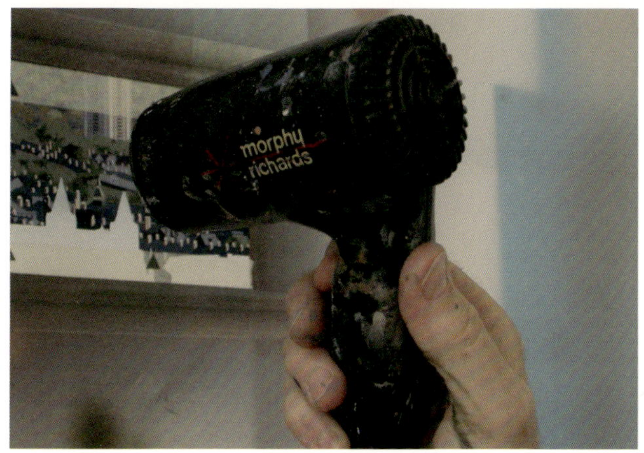

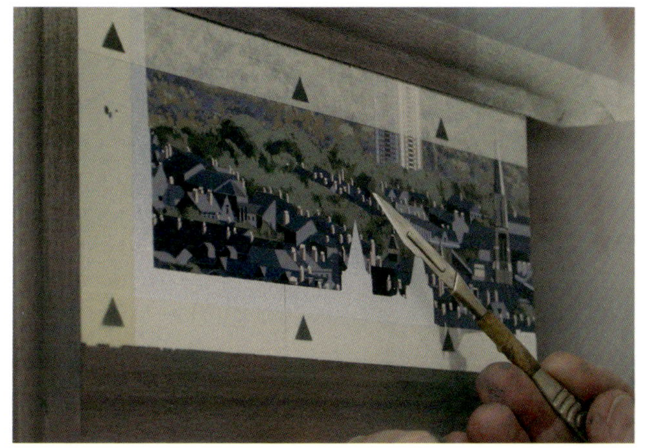

speeding up the process and enabling ever more precise individual stencils to be made. Only the tiniest redundant pieces of vinyl are now removed by hand, a process referred to as 'weeding'. Each building or group comprises, on average, 25 stencils. More elaborate structures have required far more. The waterfront Port of Liverpool Building proved the single most complex, necessitating 380 stencils. In total 22,950 stencils have been used for 'The Liverpool Cityscape' – excluding those for the landscape, foliage and water.

While the stencils are being prepared, the paint colours are identified and mixed. The same source photographs are scrutinised and a colour palette for each building, group or landscape feature determined. The colours are hand-mixed then decanted into small pots which fill the spray gun. Each pot has a colour swatch card noting its unique recipe for future use. Annotated reference drawings are printed and marked up with colour notes for the artist's use. By completion, the Cityscape contained some 700 individual colours. Blended, these produced a spectrum of many thousands.

Positioned using the grid and reference plans, the distinctive blue self-adhesive stencils are applied to the canvas and rubbed down to remove air bubbles. The canvas surrounding the spraying area is masked off for protection. A series of notches, through which triangular markers are sprayed onto the canvas, ensure that each stencil is keyed into position in relation to the previous ones used. With the appropriate colour pot attached, each section of building is sprayed, in a sequence that varies from building to building. Gradually the image emerges.

This method results in the city materialising in a series of jigsaw-like segments across the white background. As the gaps are filled, the relationship between these pieces becomes clear. The illusion of reality, of recognisable streets that can be navigated, crystallises.

The stencils' application and removal, and Johnson's subsequent blow-drying of the paint with a domestic hairdryer, is a startlingly harsh, physical procedure, at odds with the intricacies of the overall process and the apparent delicacy of the painting's surface. Inevitably, too, the spraying sometimes leaves tiny areas of bare canvas or 'bleed' at the margins of each colour. These are touched-in by hand, using a very fine brush, usually by Sheila Johnson, Ben's wife, and one of his assistants.

Johnson's approach results in the creation of thousands of exquisite computer-generated line drawings and hand-annotated colour diagrams of each building. These have decorated the studio walls throughout the project, creating not merely a sketchbook but an overall campaign plan for the sections currently being painted. To outsiders, the spectacle is mind-boggling.

Despite the immense detail in his paintings, the absence of people is something that is all the more conspicuous in this Cityscape, since Liverpool's character and its population are inseparable. Without doubt, those living and working in the city have played a vital role in the creation of this painting, by supporting and inspiring the artist throughout. That *The Liverpool Cityscape* should act as a catalyst for activities that will 'put the people back into the painting' is the aim of the artist and all those involved in this project, during 2008 at the Walker Art Gallery and at its future home at the Museum of Liverpool.

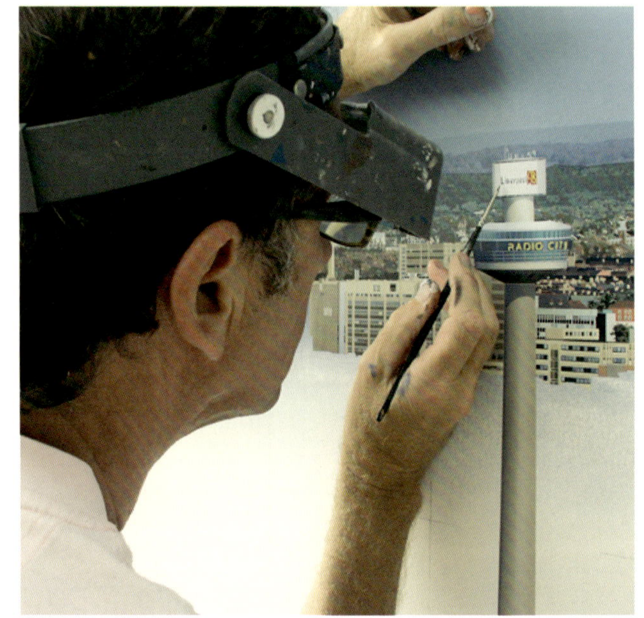

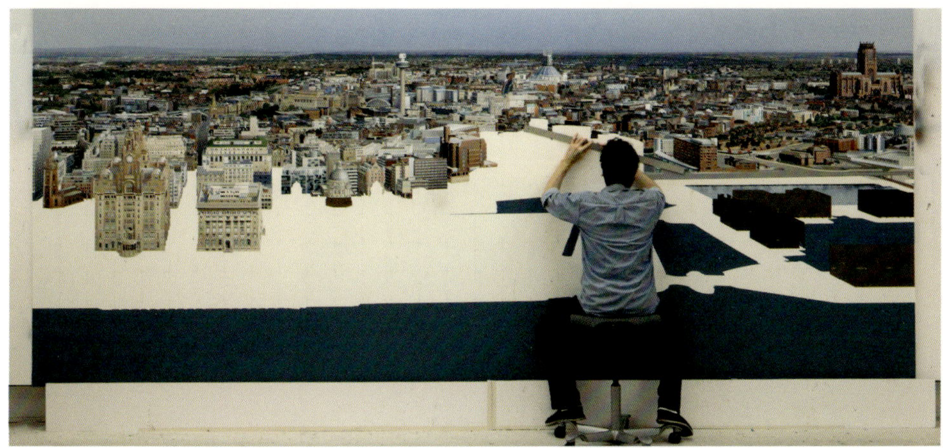
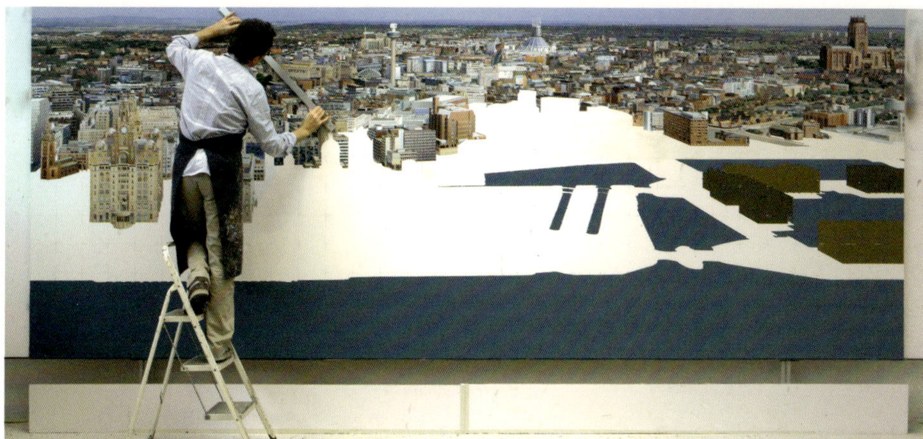
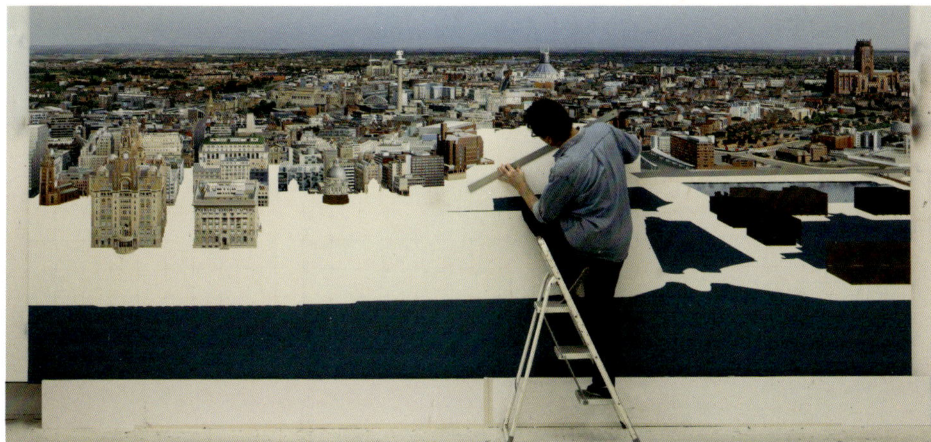
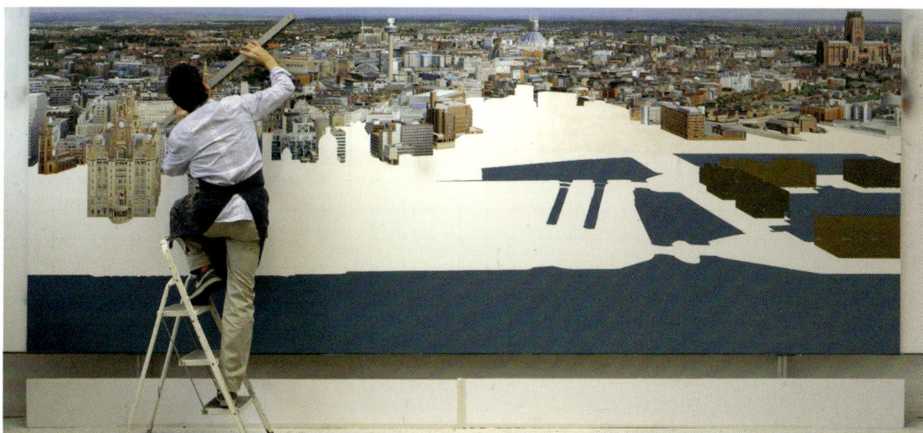
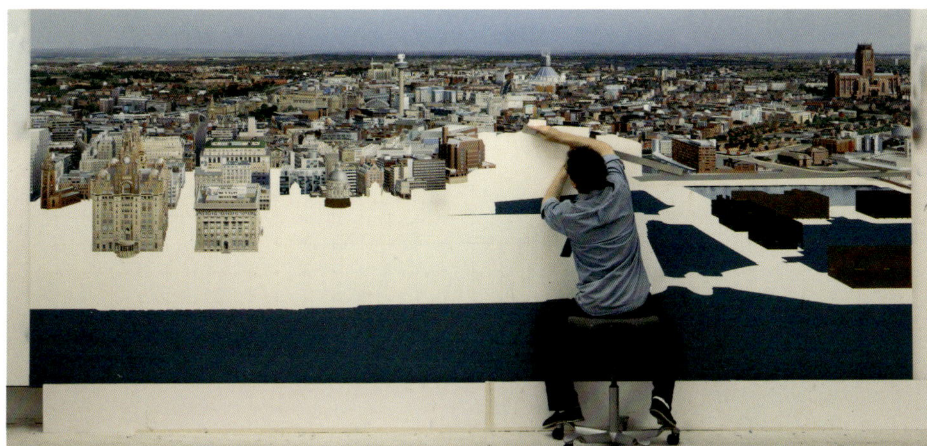
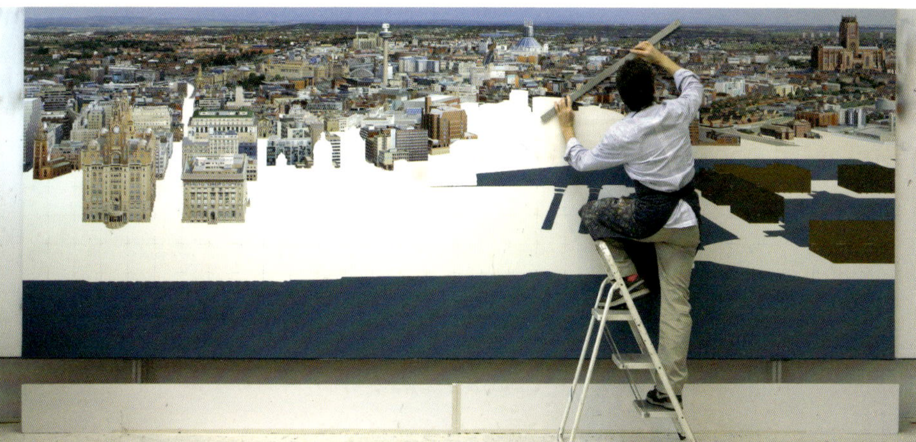

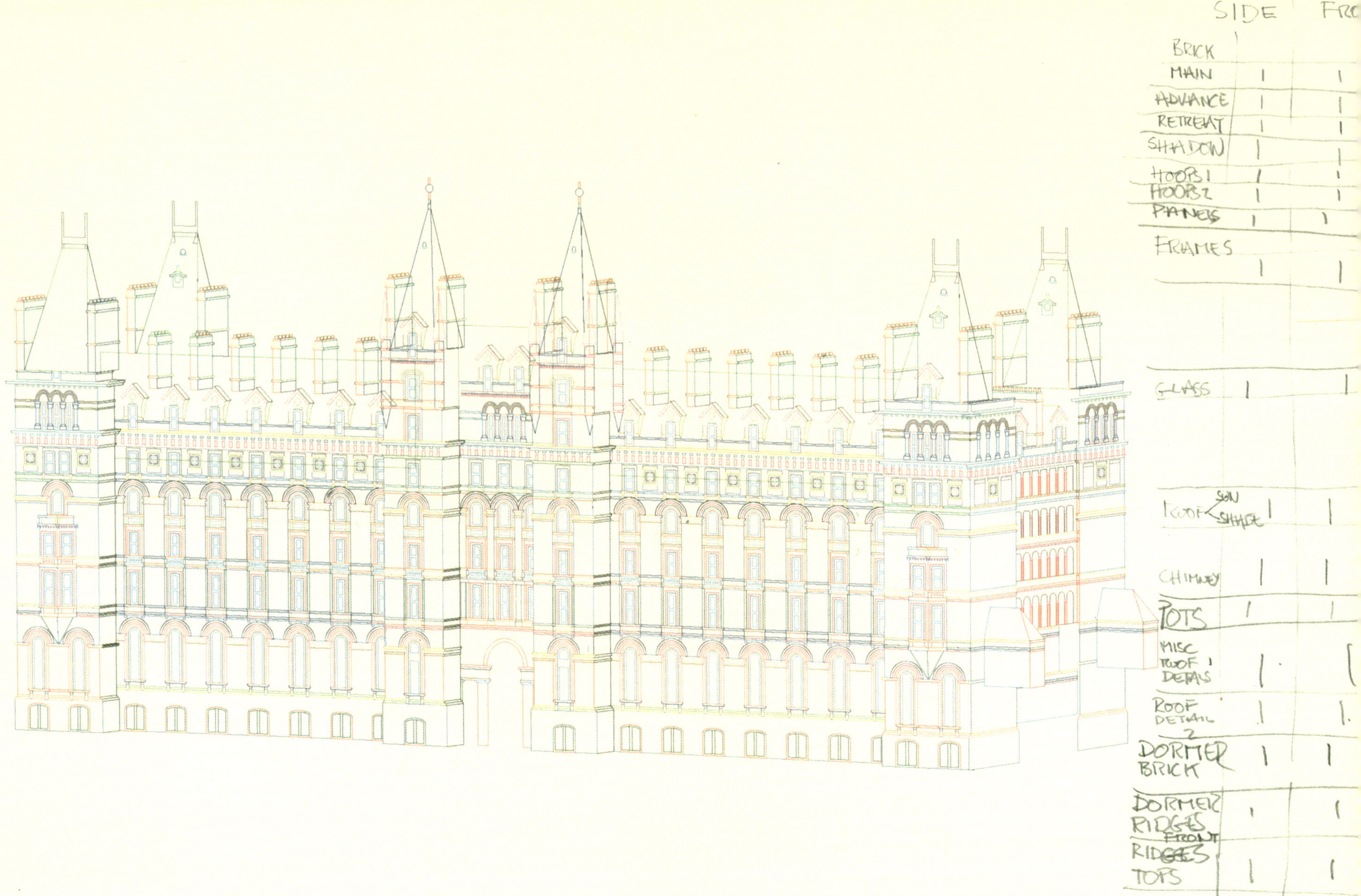

Computer drawing and colour separation for the former Lime Street station hotel

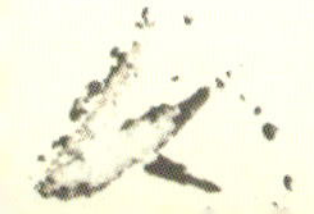

...me st. hotel draw (col)
23 FEB '07 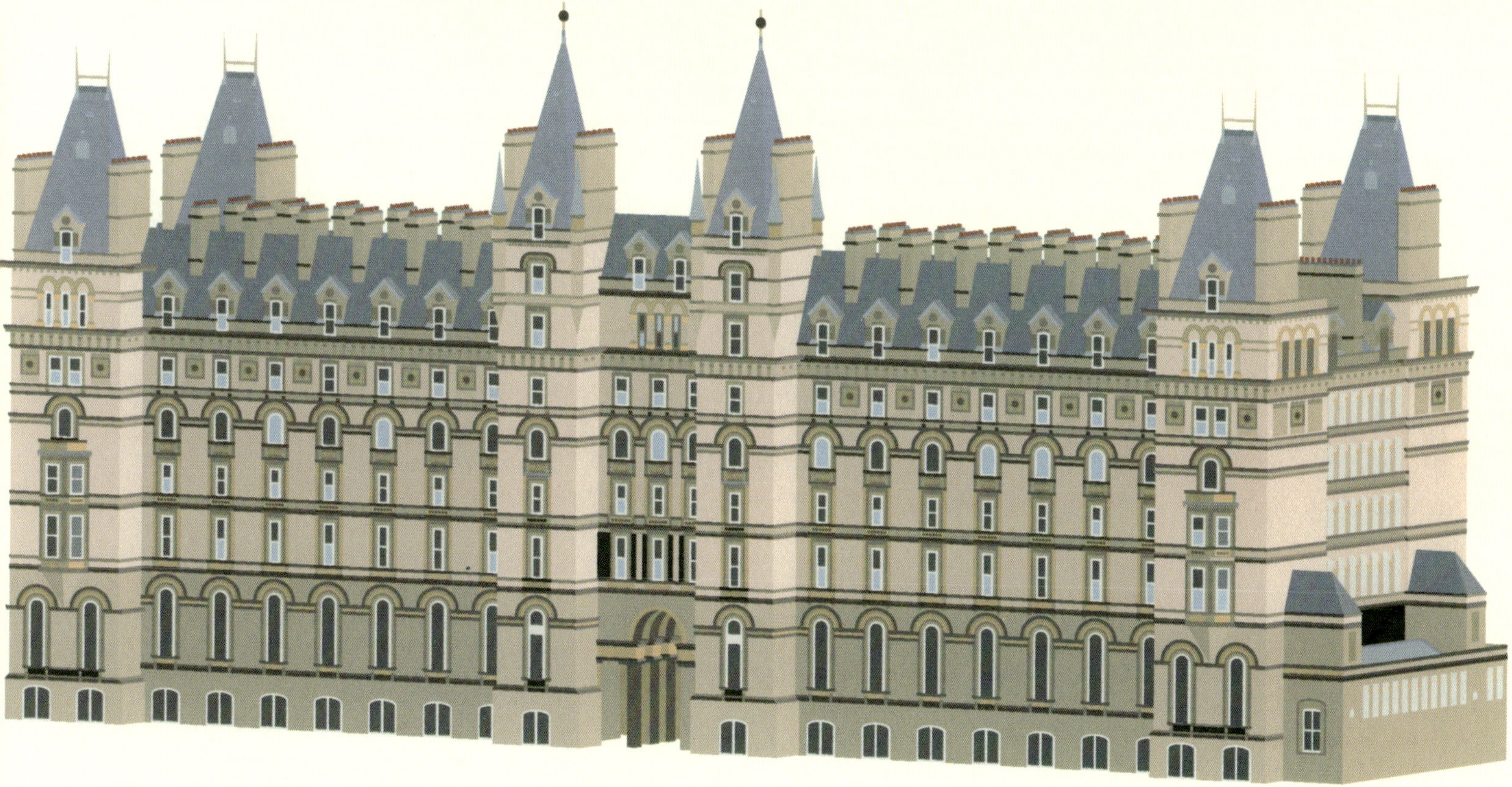
1 Tower front roofs
2 Tower side roofs
3 Main front roofs 1
4 Main facade front face 1
5 Main side chimney stacks
6 Main facade side face 1
7 Main facade front face 2
8 Main facade side face 2
9 Tower front face 1
10 Side windows 1
11 Tower side face 1
12 Tower side face 2
13 Tower front face 2
14 Front windows outer frame 1
15 Main windows outer frame 2
16 Main front win outer frame 3
17 Main front win outer frame 4
18 Main frame
19 Main f
20 Tower panel
21 Tower
22 Tower
23 Tower
24 Main edging
25 Glass
26 Glass
27 Main
28 Main
29 Tower
30 main upper
31 Tower
32 Tower edging
33 Tower
34 Tower

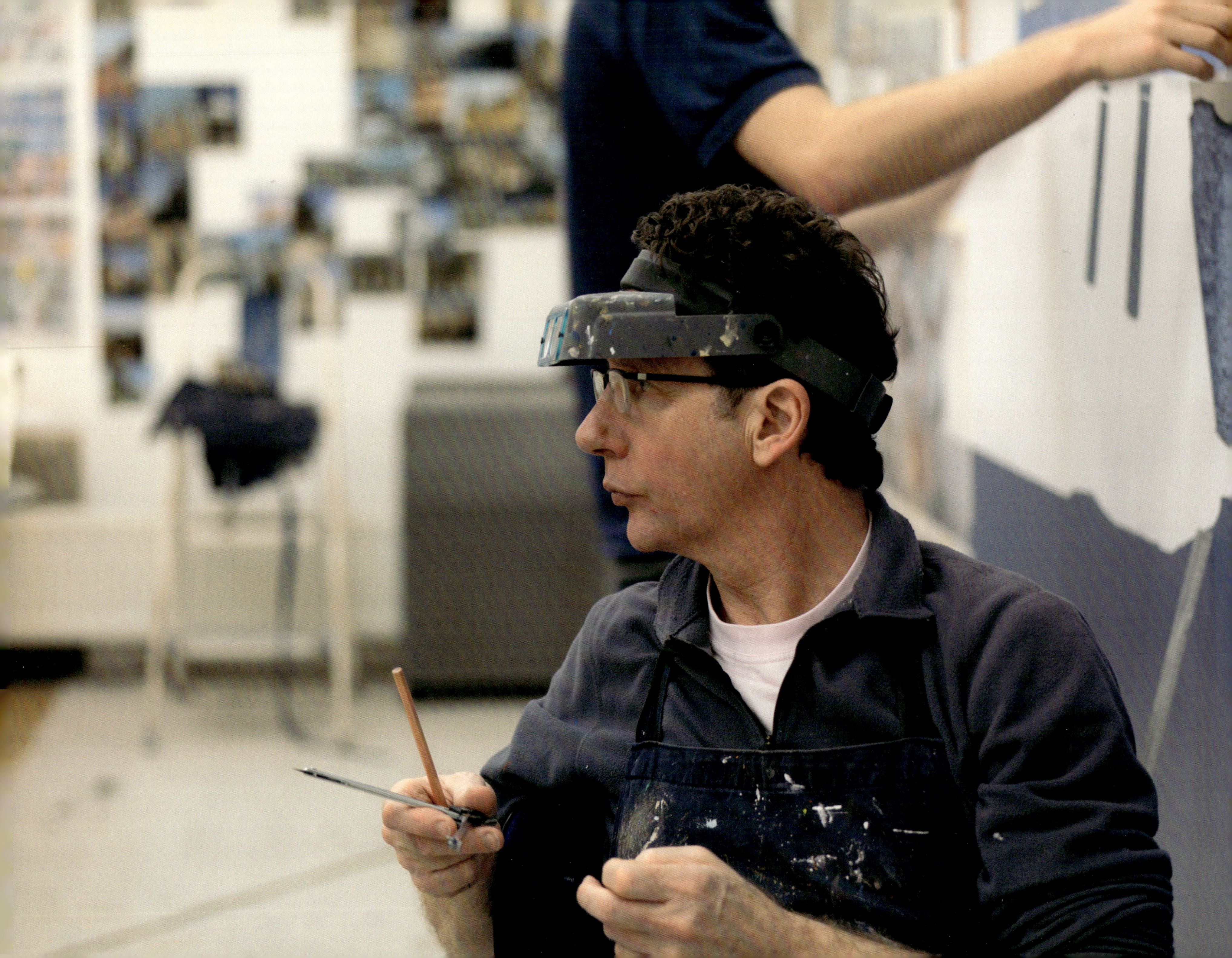

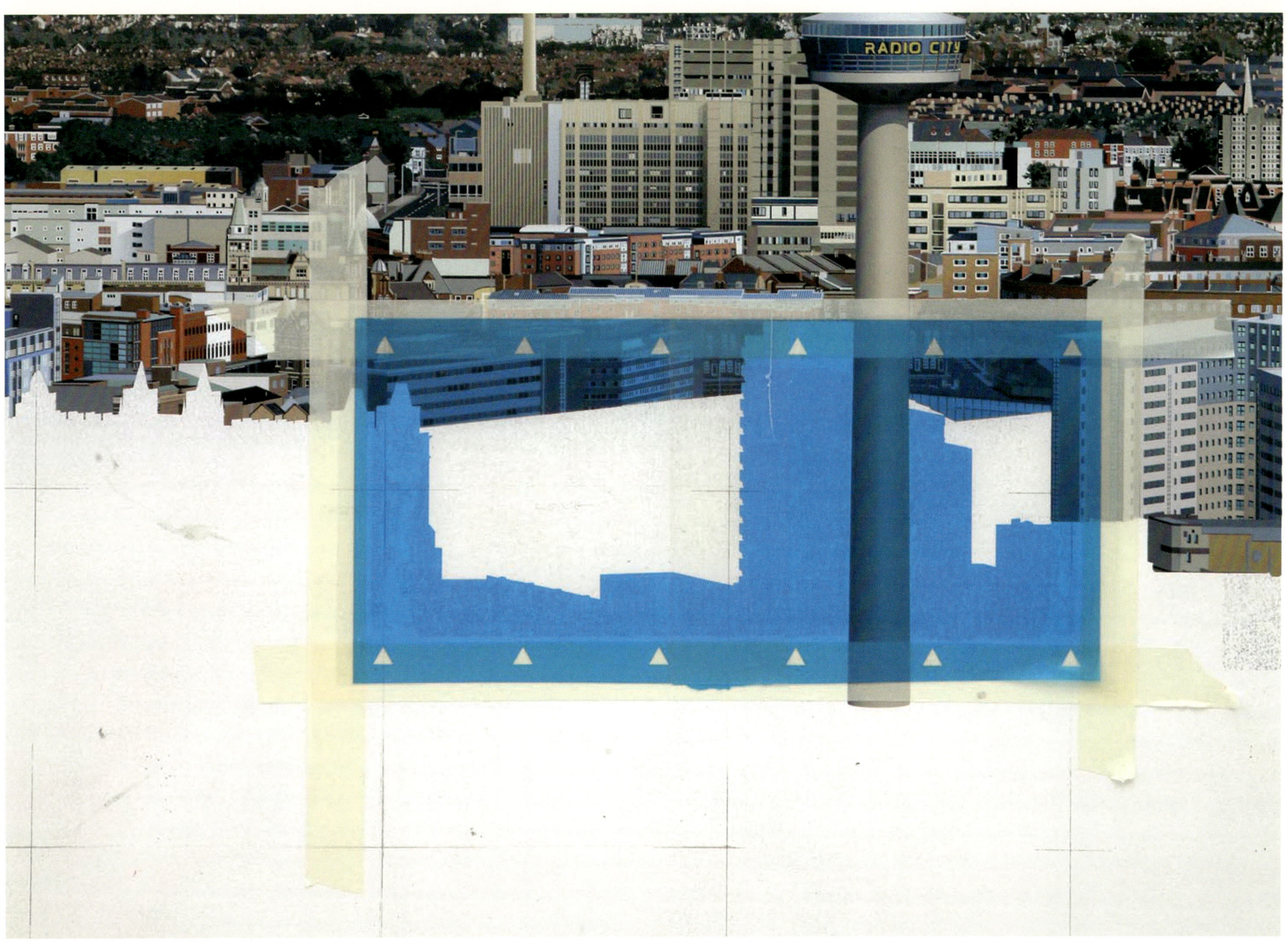

RADIO CITY

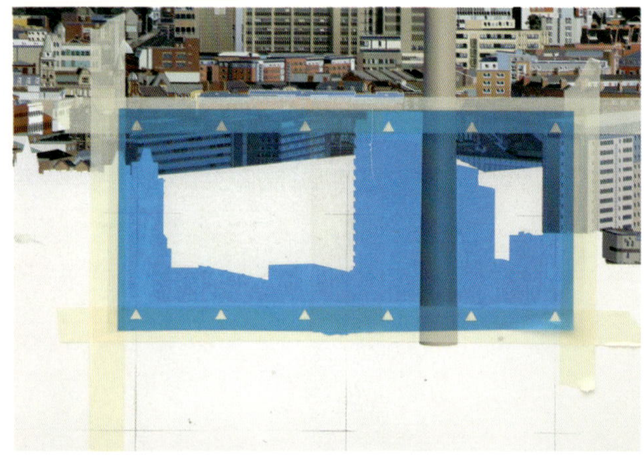
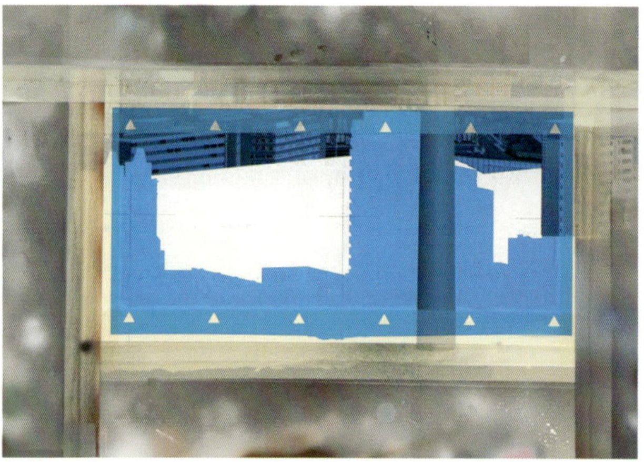
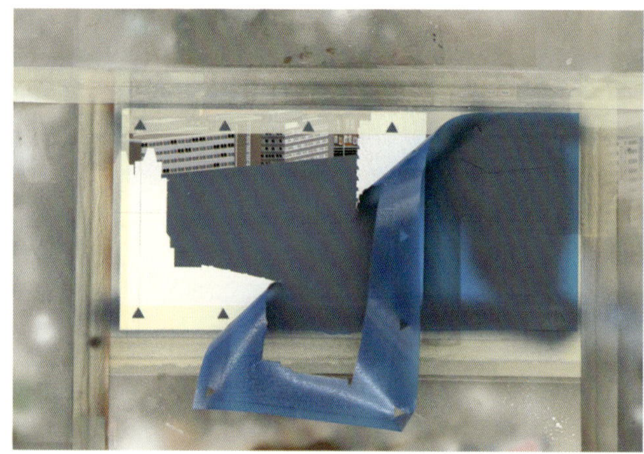
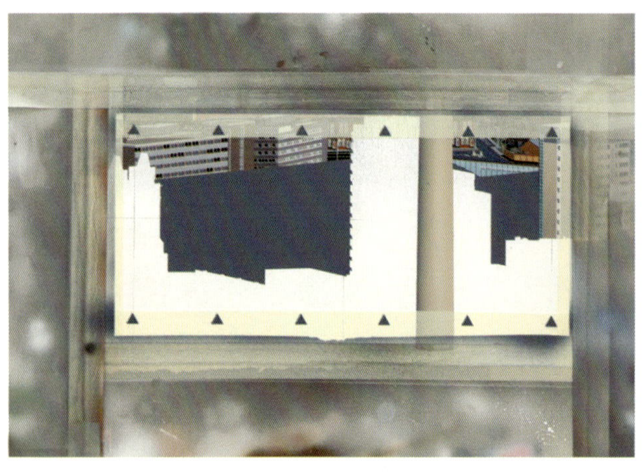
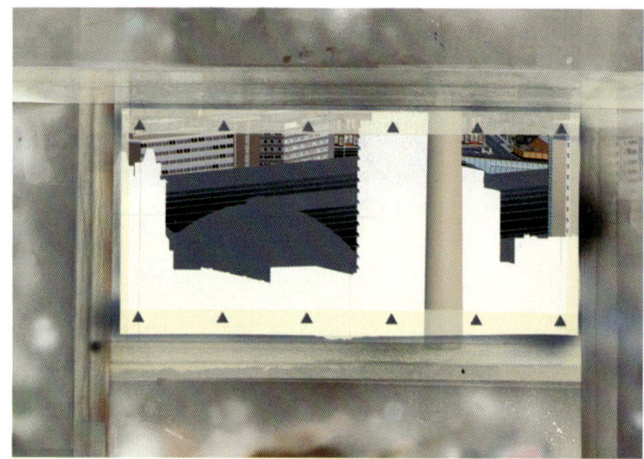
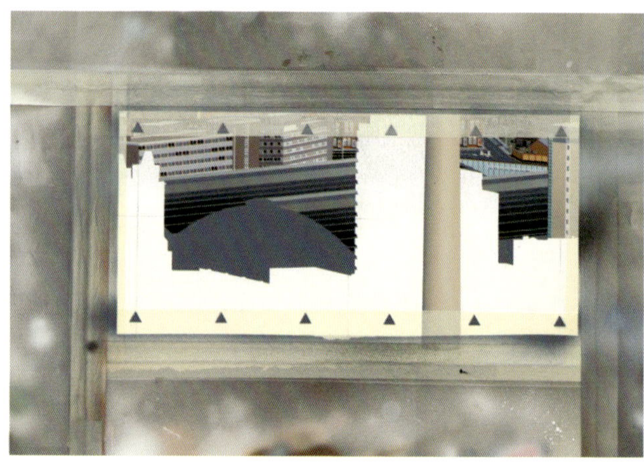
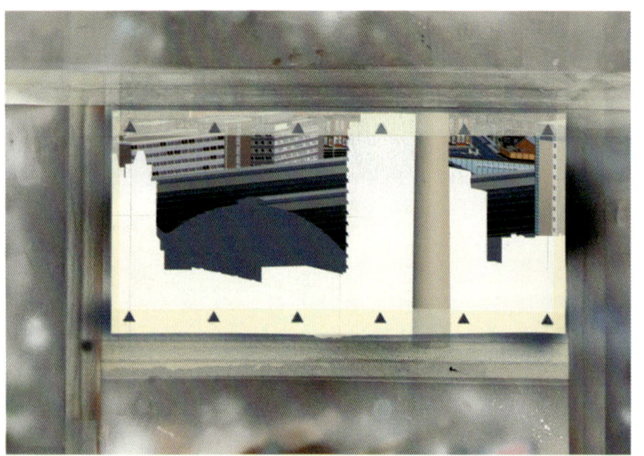
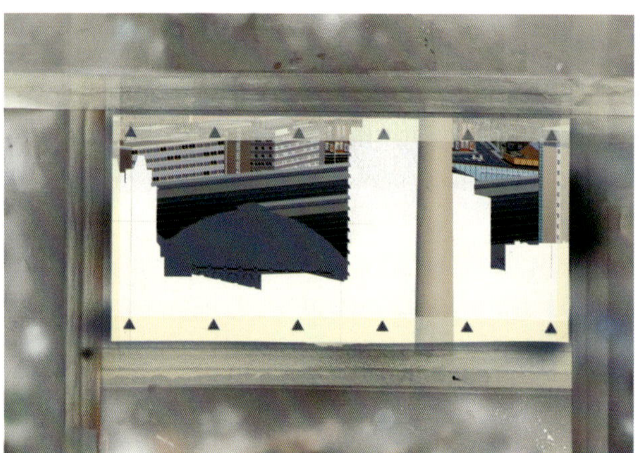
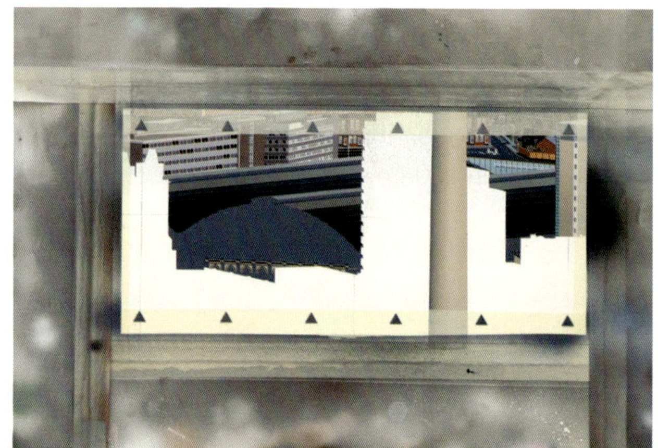

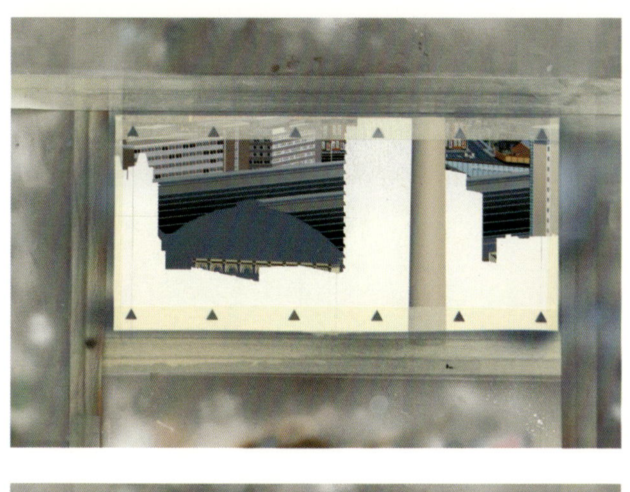
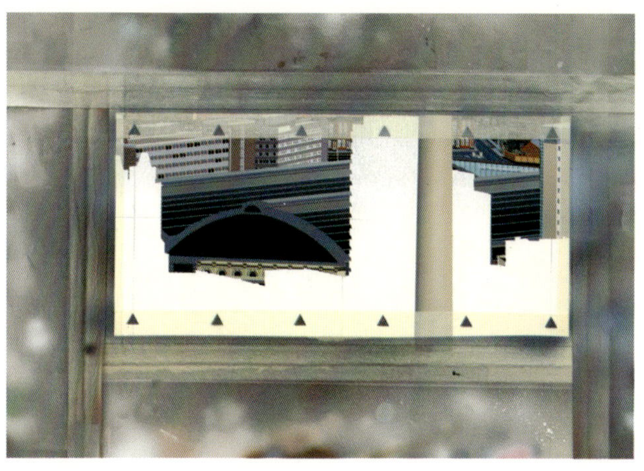
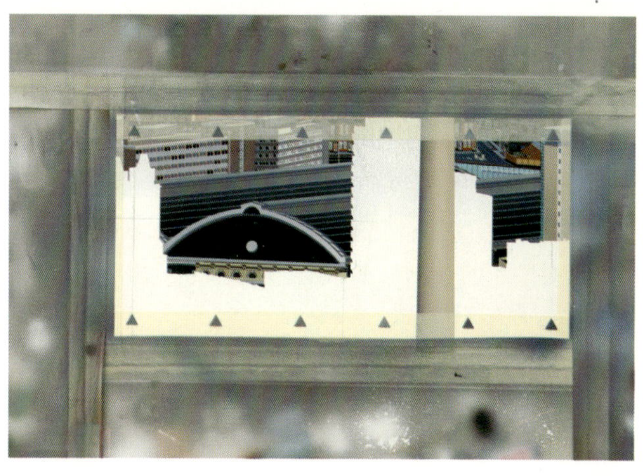
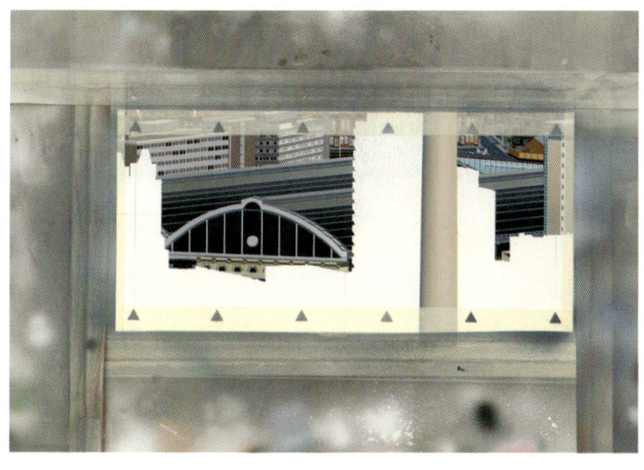
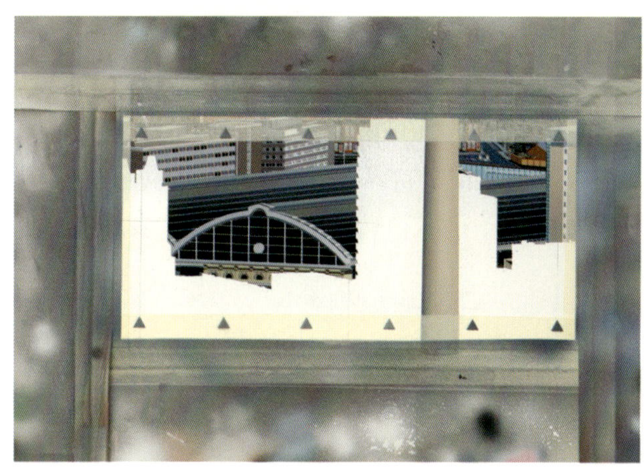
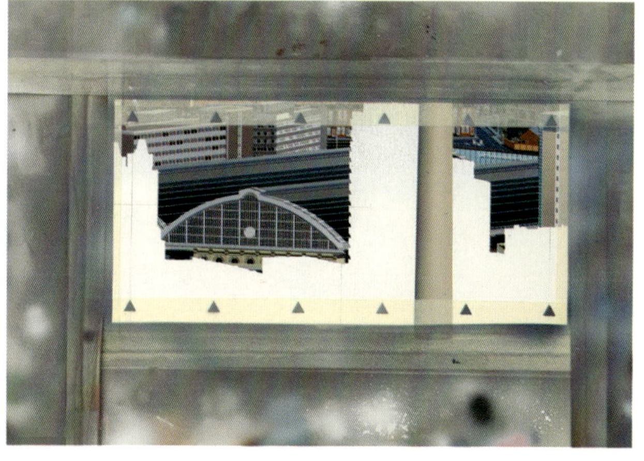
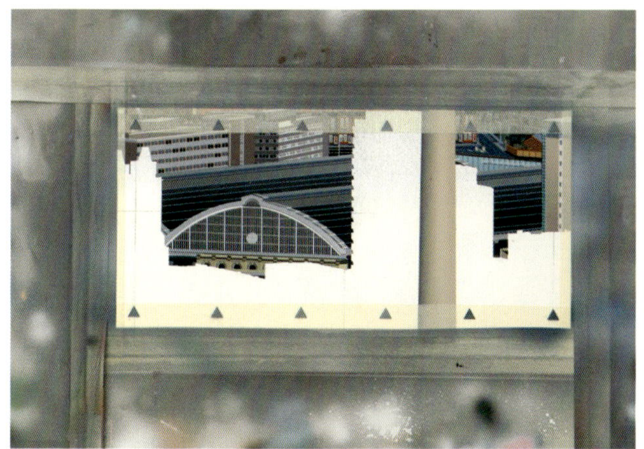
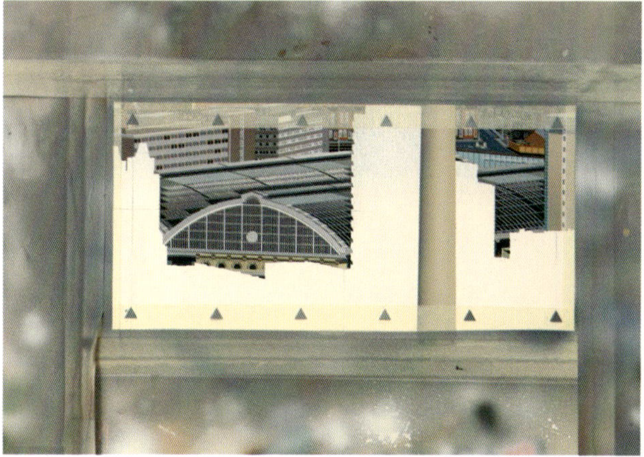
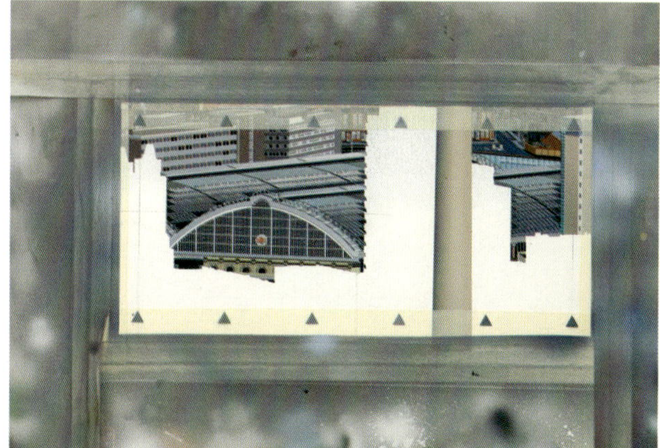

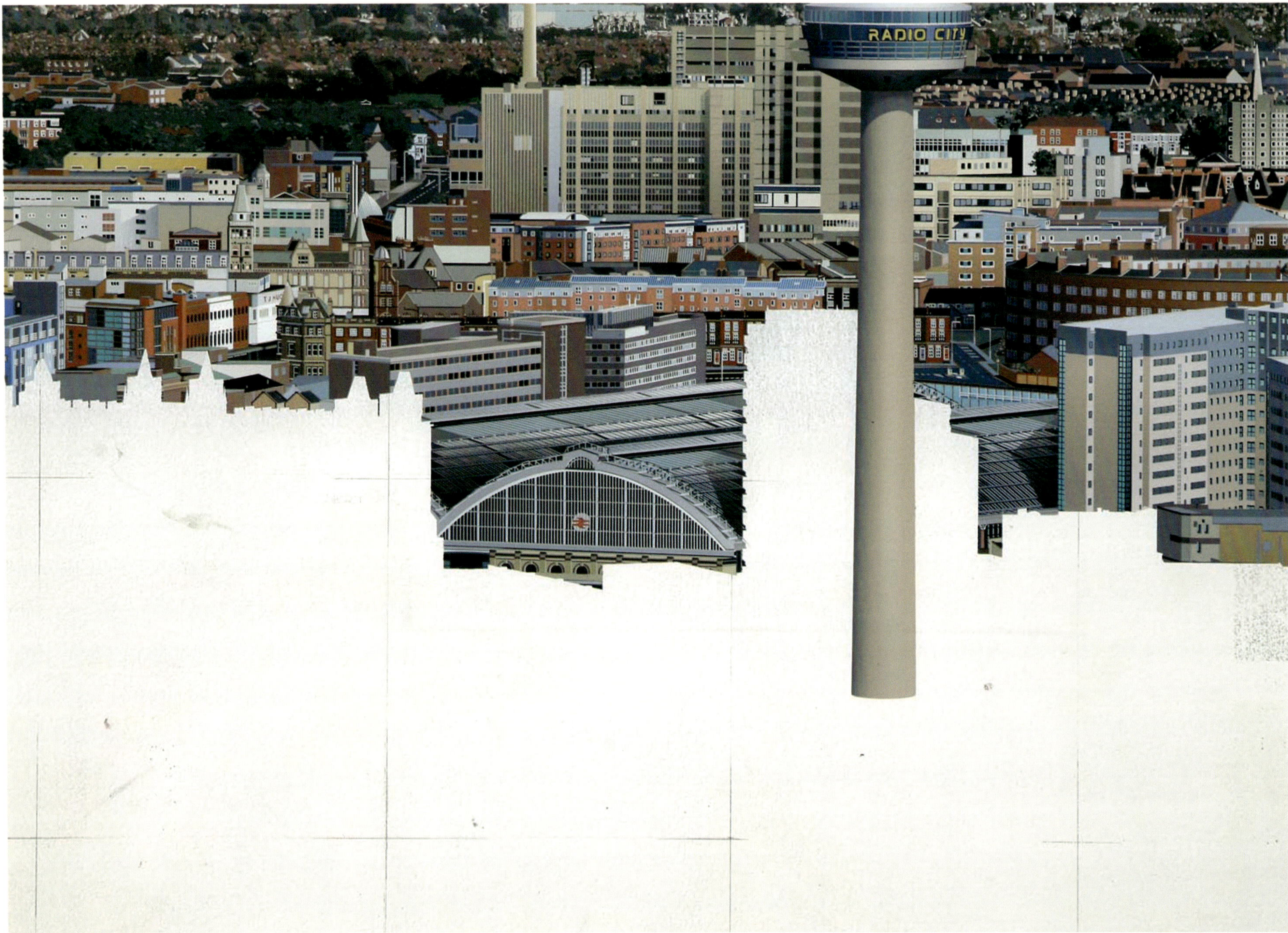
RADIO CITY

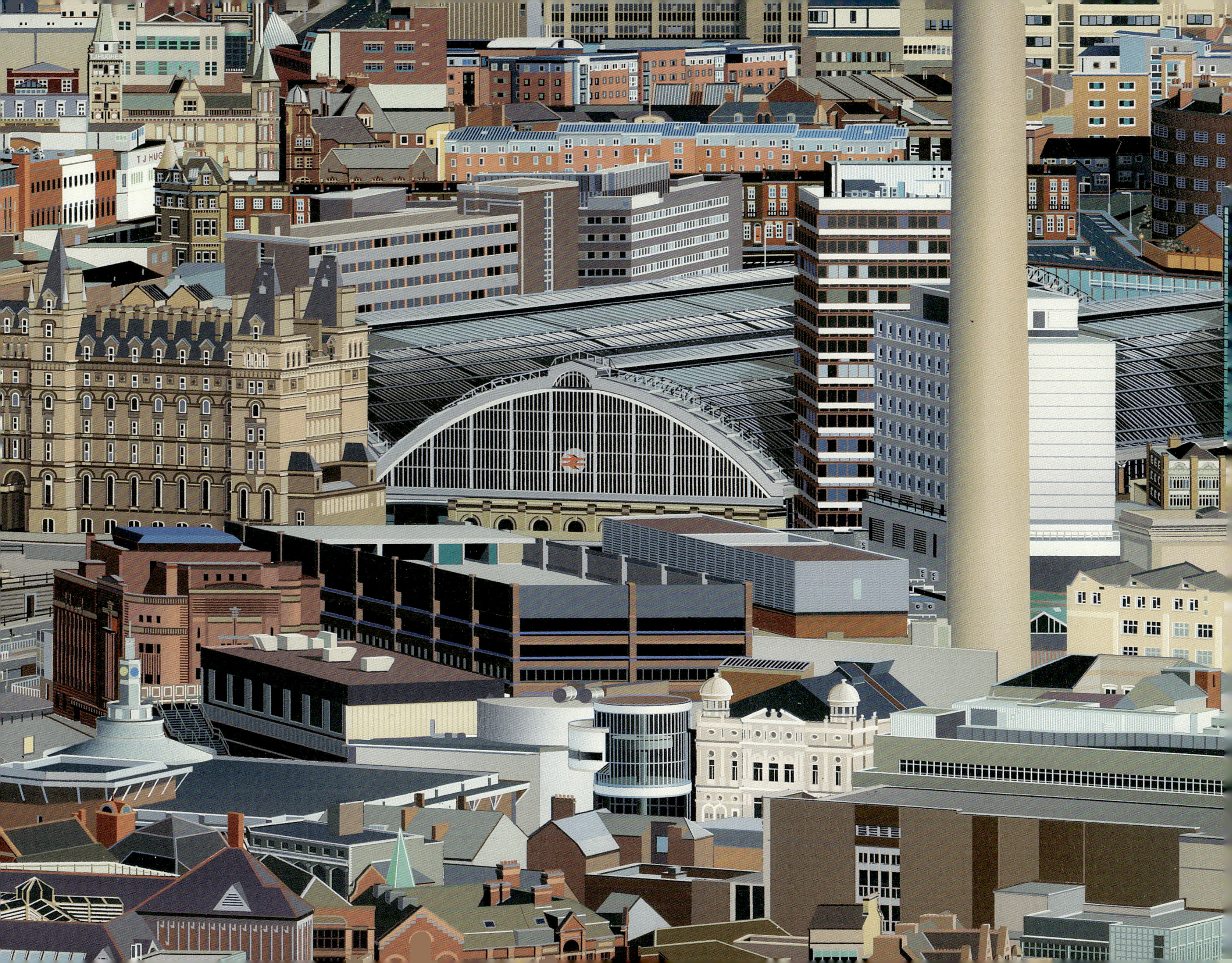

T J HUG

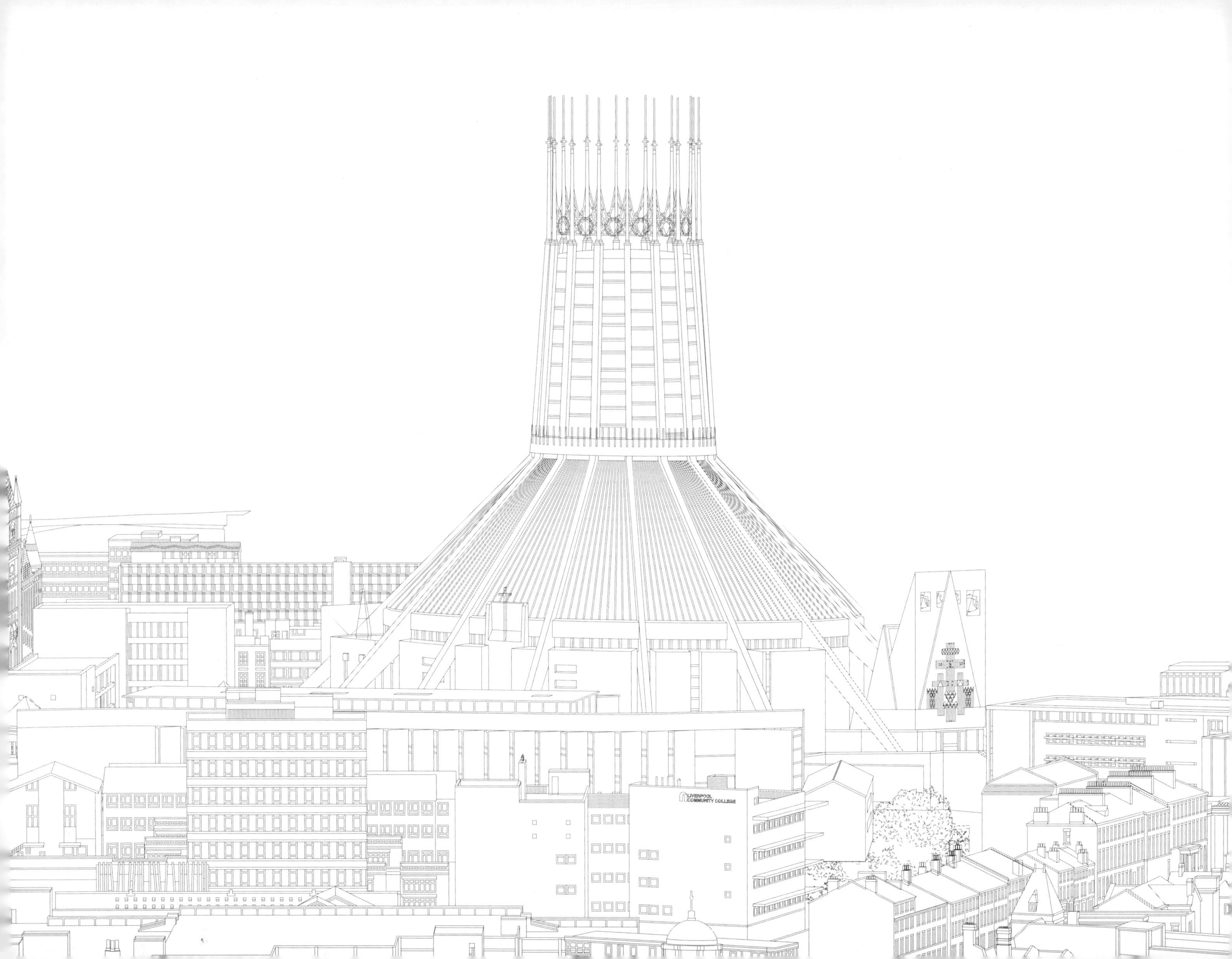

LIVERPOOL
COMMUNITY COLLEGE

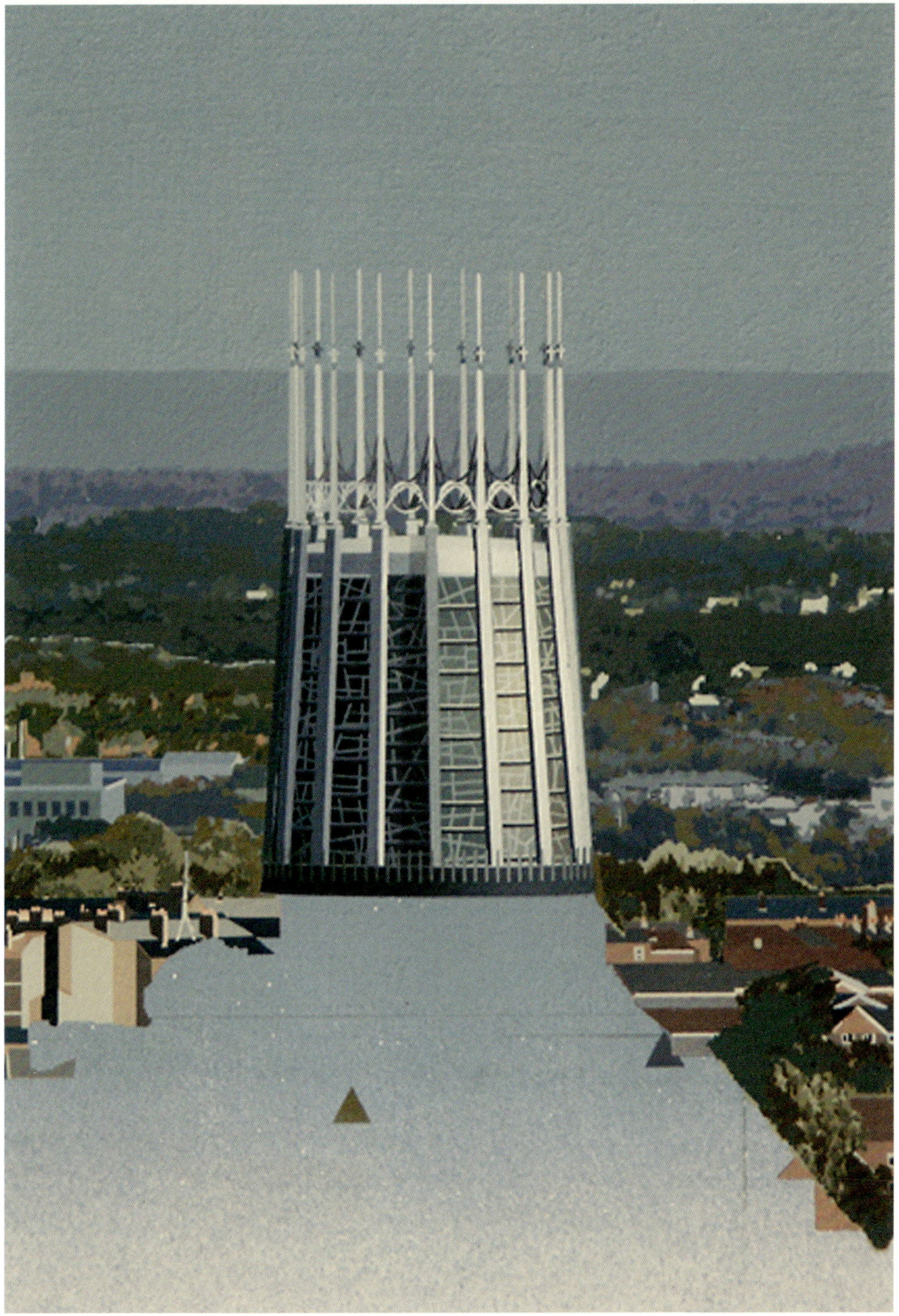

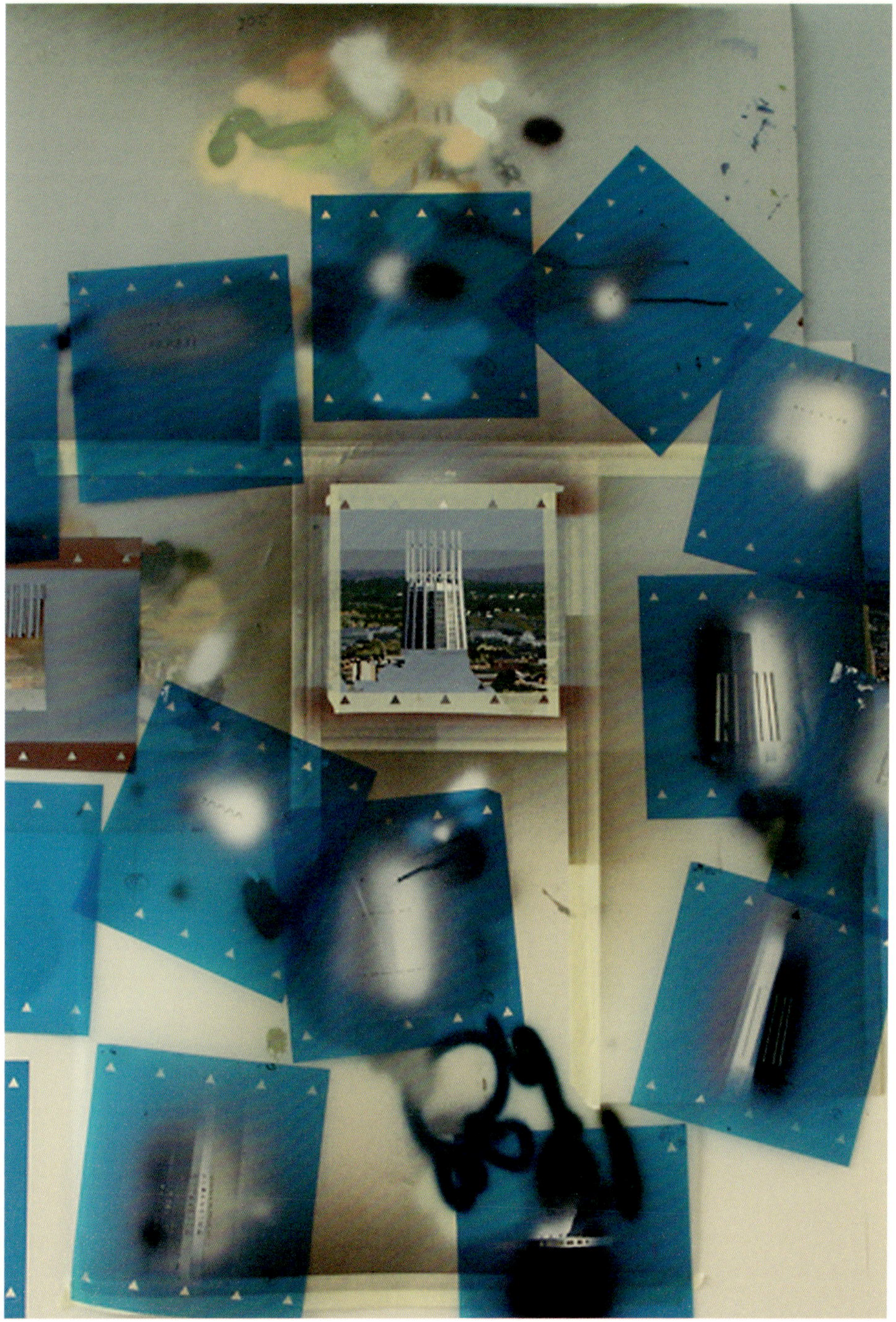

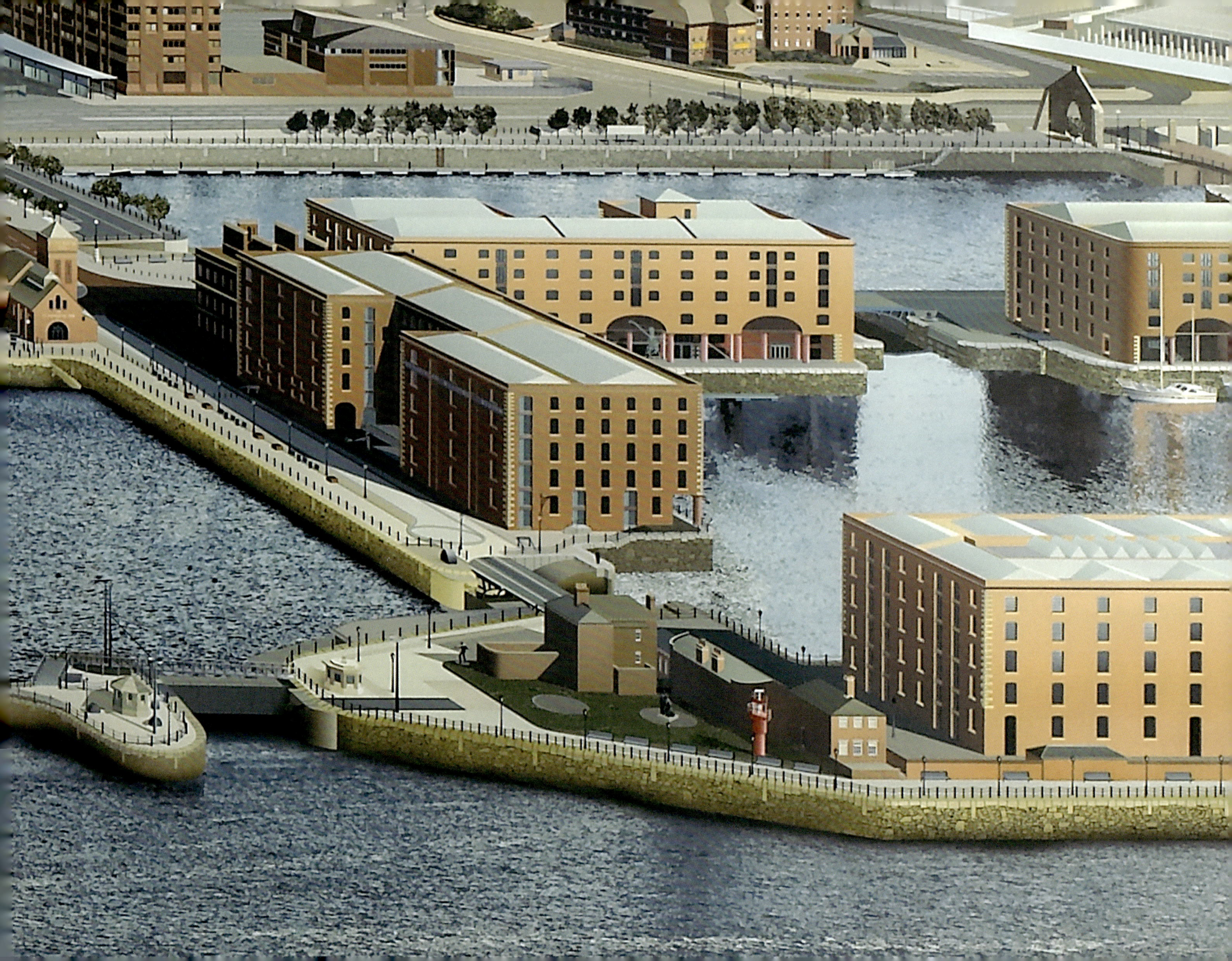

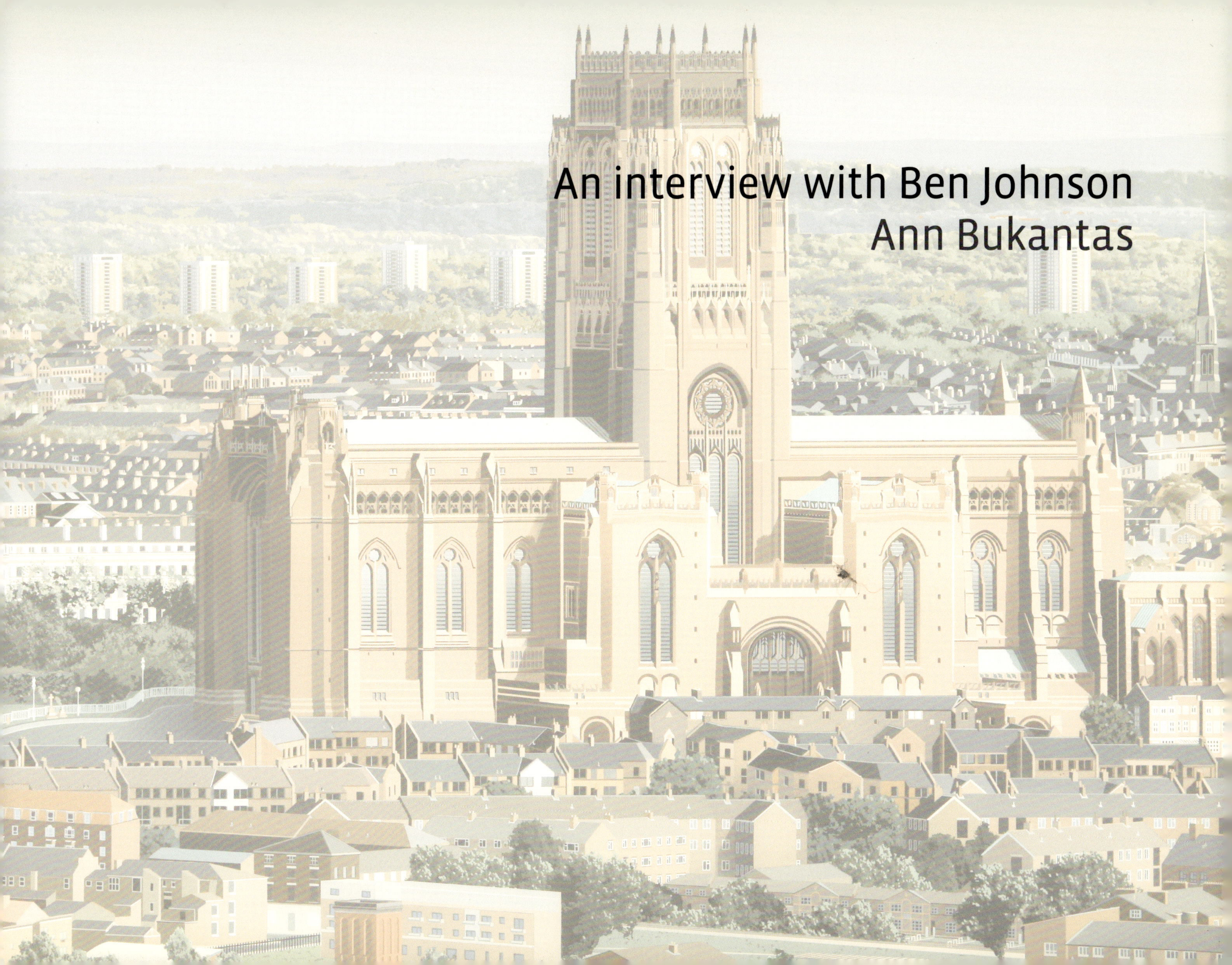
An interview with Ben Johnson
Ann Bukantas

Tell us about your studio team and their importance to the way that you work.

At one time I would have brought in assistants to back me up and to execute things that I hadn't got time to do. On *The Liverpool Cityscape* I've matured in my use of the studio and recognised the interdependence and the individual talents of people that I employ. From the beginning I had a vision that had to be realised. To do that I needed talents which I neither had the time nor ability to master and I brought in people with their own skills. We came together as individuals contributing to one goal. I became the coordinator and on many occasions I accepted images or solutions that I wouldn't have come up with on my own. I have learnt from each of those people and feel humbled by their skills and willingness to work as part of a team. Without them I couldn't have achieved the end result.

The computer-driven cutter that you use seems to have revolutionised the way you work. Would a painting of this scale and complexity have been possible without it?

Yes, but if I total up the hours that have been put into this painting it is approximately eighteen years. Without the aid of the technology, which has done all the cutting of the stencils, we could multiply that by five. The painting could have been realised but nobody would have taken it on. We can leave the studio at the end of the day and leave a machine cutting, a form of intricate cutting that we could never possibly have done, not without going blind or crazy.

Why did you accept *The Liverpool Cityscape* commission?

It was the realisation of a dream to make paintings – cityscapes – that had a social relevance, paintings that would be put into a public arena where the people of the city could interact with the finished object.

Do you feel part of an historic tradition of artists recording cities?

I am not a recorder of cities or a documentary painter. I am obsessed – and it may seem strange – with people above and beyond everything else. Historically there have been people that have recorded cities but many of them I don't really want to be associated with. I use architecture as a symbol of people's ambitions and conflicts and questioning of society. I believe I'm part of a growing group of people that are questioning the nature of cities and an understanding of cities as being an understanding of the individual operating within society.

The city is about people and Liverpool is about people and that's all that matters. The painting is for the people of Liverpool to stand in front of and give their voice to all those lonely, deserted streets that I have portrayed in a slightly surreal atmosphere.

What role do you feel the Residency at the Walker Art Gallery will play in the creation of the painting?

From the very beginning the Residency has been the cherry on the cake. It's been the possibility of offering my work up for criticism. For some it'll just be a 'fancy' picture. For others it may be an opportunity to discuss areas they know and love and consider what the city of Liverpool means to them. It could be, I hope, an object for argument, where some people may say, 'Why on the earth has somebody wasted three years making something that could have been a photograph?' As long as they discuss it, that's the most important thing. Above everything else I would like it to just spark a little bit of curiosity.

How important were your visits to Liverpool, taking in the city's atmosphere and speaking to local people?

I had a predisposition to like Liverpool. I grew up in North Wales, then in Chester and my very first experience of a museum was the Walker Art Gallery. And it was in the '60s. People of my generation were starting to lead the world with their youth and arrogance. My first experience of exciting contemporary life was the Cavern club. I'd also seen the very dark side of Liverpool after the war and during the Thatcher government. I saw social deprivation and injustice. The streets were not the most pleasant places to walk round.

I now go back to Liverpool and in the three years I've been visiting regularly I have seen a pride and energy. There were always the jokes, strength and independence but now there is a confidence and optimism. All of my experiences have been of meeting warm and generous people. They're very inventive and proud people. My great ambition for 2008 is that the Liverpudlians' existing pride is deepened by the smiles of the people that visit Liverpool for the first time, reinforcing their own awareness that they're living in a very special place.

What does it mean to you to be working at the Walker Art Gallery and to have your work in the gallery's collection?

I'm not really sure that this isn't still a dream and I'm not going to wake up and somebody's going to say, 'Only joking'. I can remember one coach journey from Chester Art School to Liverpool and we were talking about our ambitions as young art students. I arrogantly said I'd love to have my work in a museum one day and my friends fell about laughing. To think that I've actually got work not only in a museum but the very museum I was travelling to that day is utterly astonishing.

You sometimes manipulate or move buildings to make them visible or more prominent. Are you catering for people's expectations?

If you undertake a view of a city you have already taken on an enormous amount of artistic licence because you're filtering it through your own personality, philosophy and views. For *The Liverpool Cityscape* there are very simple changes and I haven't made many. In Liverpool, culture is out on the streets, it's in the football stadiums, it's in the sun parlours. It's a very broad culture and that's what I love. I am trying to respect the people of Liverpool and I wouldn't want to leave out some very important symbols, like the 'Three Graces', the Metropolitan and the Anglican Cathedrals. But we mustn't forget the Greek Orthodox Church and the Synagogue. Chinese culture is very significant – I've raised, just slightly, the arch into Chinatown and I'm putting in the very first Muslim prayer centre. I'm still sure a hundred people are going to tell me I haven't put them in, and I am sorry.

Did you aim to depict the city at a particular time of year or day?

The time of year or day didn't really matter. The photographs have been taken almost on a twelve-month basis throughout the year. I've tried to choose a light between 12 noon and 8 o'clock in the evening with a light coming from the south and the south-west. I've painted Liverpool always in a very strong light, often more like a winter light that is very cruel and telling. Each building is picked out almost in a spotlight. Superficially the painting could look slightly bland because I've got no large areas of shadow, no clouds going over and that's a risk. Artistically it would have been much easier to make a dramatic painting by putting it in a dramatic lighting situation. But I wanted to throw an equal amount of light on every building so that people can find a little bit of their own history in a pool of light.

Did Liverpool emerge as having a particular colour palette?

It did. Sandstone is very important for the city. Liverpool is dominated by the Anglican Cathedral on the right and the city is built on the edges of Cheshire, on sandstone, clay, red. The red is important but alongside it there is often a grey sky over Liverpool. The architects of Liverpool have also worked well with blues and cold colours. Within the studio there's a joke that I've made it a pink and blue city. They say, 'Do you think the people of Liverpool will like this much pink?' It's not pink, it's sandstone.

Were you nervous about tackling a city that provokes such passionate feeling from its citizens?

No, because anything that doesn't create a passionate feeling shouldn't exist. We all need passionate feelings, so I warmed to passion.

Are people's reactions to *The Liverpool Cityscape* important to you?

They're very important. I don't mind if people don't like the painting. I would like people at least to respect the fact that I've made the best effort I can in my own limited way. What I've most enjoyed are the people who have been enthusiastic about the painting. Even if they haven't, if it's moved them enough to talk about Liverpool and their own experience, then that's given me satisfaction. I get no greater pleasure than somebody telling me that that's where their parents were married, or a story about the city. The people of Liverpool are good story-tellers. I would like this to be a springboard for a thousand stories.

What were the challenges of painting a city that had so much development going on in it?

It's a continuing problem. I'm within two months of finishing the painting but there are certain very significant areas in the foreground, and therefore they're very large, that still have question marks hanging over them. It's not through lack of commitment from the council, the architects or the developers. In 2008 there is some economic uncertainty. Are certain buildings going ahead or not? Can I leave the foreground of the painting as an undeveloped building site? That wouldn't do justice to the city. What risks should I take? My painting is not a *capriccio*, a fantasy. It may be an alternative view but it's meant to be based in reality. Do I leave buildings in or out? It's a difficult decision because I know that my painting is to last several hundred years. There are many discussions still to be had.

Your photographs of Liverpool form a remarkable visual resource in their own right. What do you see the future of these as being?

The archive is enormous. There are two archives in a way. One is the archive of the city that was essential to make the painting. Then there's the archive of the making of the painting. For the first, I've walked each street that I have represented within the painting taking photographs; not the artistic type that some photographers might, but if we put them all together it's a very useful document for understanding a city at an important point of change in its physical development.

The second part is the drawings. Every single building within the Cityscape has been reconstructed involving an enormous amount of artistic input. They are beautiful objects. I don't know what's going to happen to the archive but I think it should be kept together. I don't believe that there is any single painting in the history of art that has ever been so well documented in its manufacture.

Do you have a favourite building in the city?

I love each building and just walking around the city. One that's often overlooked is Oriel Chambers. This was the inspiration for John Root, a young architect from America in the late nineteenth century. He lived with relatives in Liverpool and his whole future was shaped by watching Oriel Chambers going up. It was the first all-steel building in Europe. It was truly inspirational. In Chicago, when he started practising as an architect, he used it as his inspiration for forming the aesthetic of the city, which again informed and led New York. Liverpool, really, helped to form those two major cities aesthetically. In certain Liverpool streets you see the quality of building that it would be hard to find in any other city in the world. I've isolated one but it's only an example of many fine buildings.

The Cityscape will eventually hang in the Museum of Liverpool, a museum of city history. Does it matter whether it hangs in an art gallery or a social history museum?

There is a story I quote often. Somebody once said to me, 'I know you. You're Ben Johnson the painter.' I replied, 'Yes. I didn't realise anybody knew me.' And they said, 'Of course I know you, your work is extraordinary.' I responded, 'Thank you. That's very kind of you.' Then the person said to me, 'No, I didn't say I *like* the work. It's extraordinary.'

I'm conscious that I've devoted three years of my own work and forty years of experience to making this painting with my team. This is an eighteen-year painting. I would like anybody to stand in front of it and say, 'What an extraordinary work'. Some people are going to walk away and say, 'I don't like it, but it was extraordinary'. Others will use it as a way of remembering Liverpool or having their own view of the city reawakened, rekindled, formed. I would love children to stand in front of it and for it to become part of their heritage, part of their memory of childhood.

What was the biggest challenge of working on this project?

To get it finished. To try and realise my concept for this big view of Liverpool. The problem's been seeing the idea through to the end without compromising on my initial ambition.

How do you feel about *The Liverpool Cityscape* now it's nearing completion?

It's the good, the bad and the ugly. The ugly bit is my inability to deal with very serious social issues. The picture is too pretty in many ways, too clean and pure. My painting is one of many views of the city that say 'Liverpool is an important place'. It's got important individuals with equally important lives, whether it's a simple, humble life or a grand, loud life. All I've done is to show the shells that the snails have left behind but it's the snails that are living and breathing and crawling.

Have you enjoyed working on *The Liverpool Cityscape?*

It's been wonderful. People say, 'How can you go into the studio for three years knowing exactly what you're going to do every day?' Each day brings a new challenge because every single part of the painting is unique in its own right. Every day's work has been like making a new painting.

Do you feel you've done justice to the city that you've seen?

No, I haven't. It's a dismal failure because the people are what make Liverpool. I've already referred to the snail and the shell. Mine is the empty shell, which may have some decorative value. It's what's alive inside the shell that matters and I hope I have offered a catalyst for involvement.

Ben Johnson was speaking at his home in London on 9 January 2008

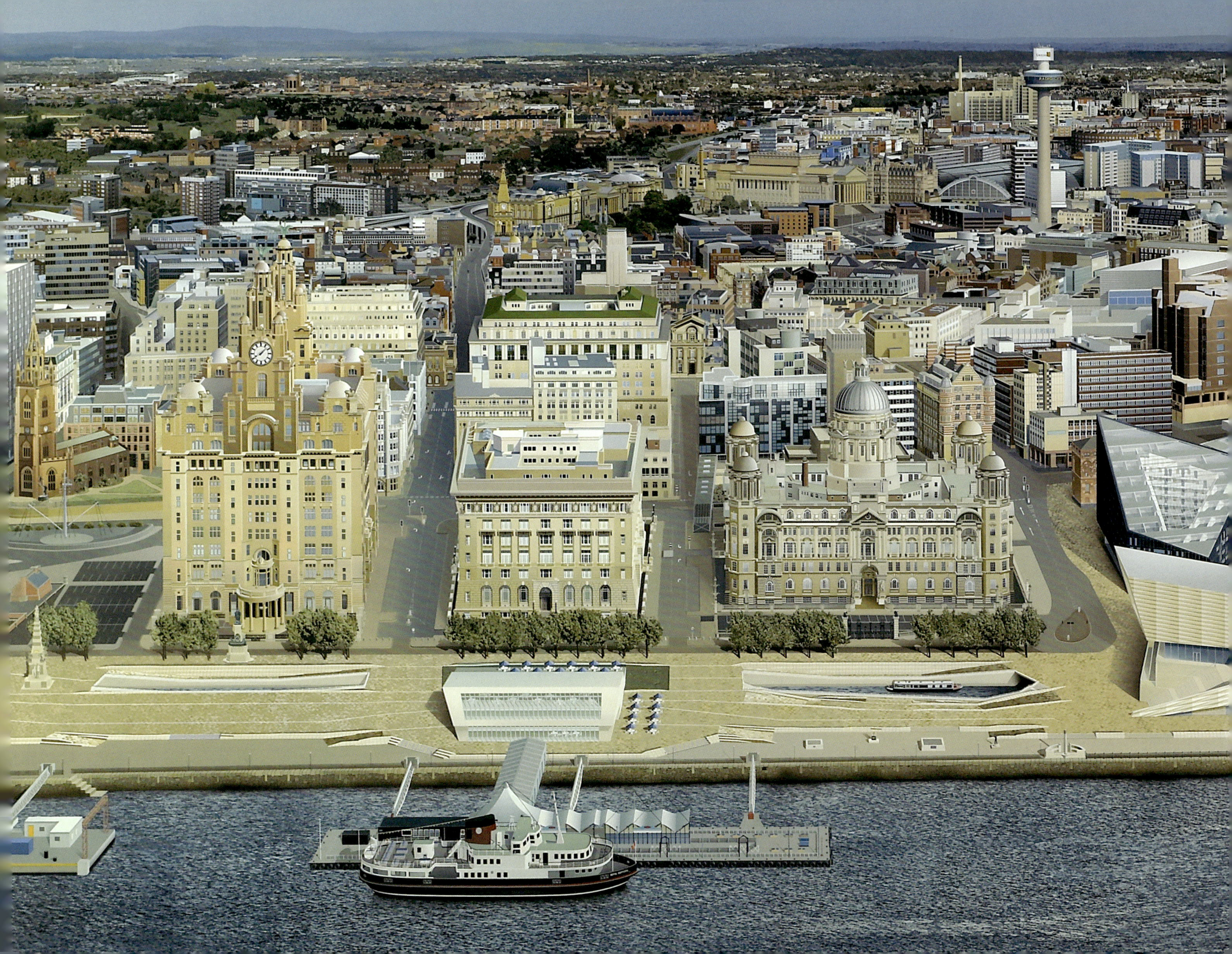

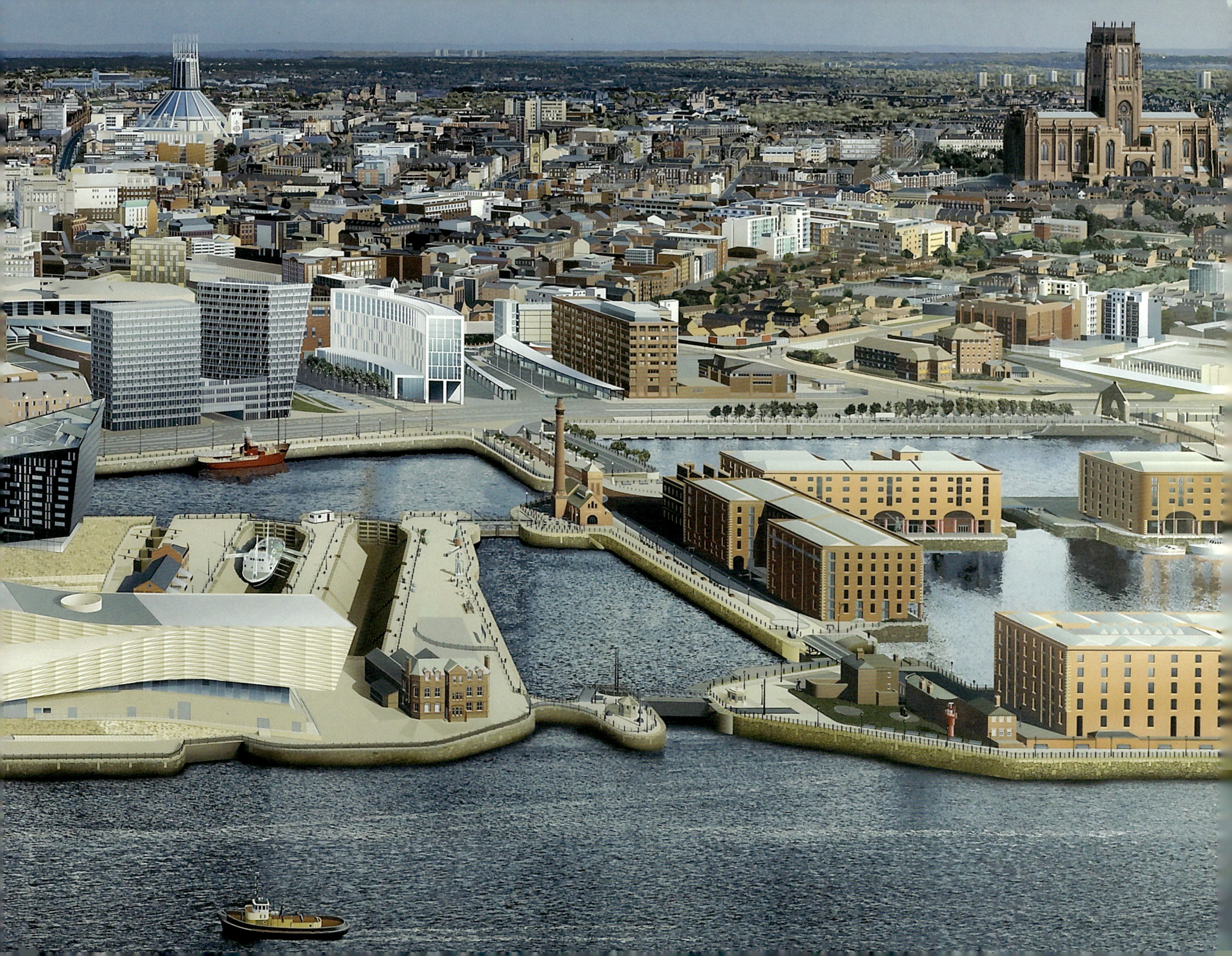

Sponsorship acknowledgments

The Liverpool Cityscape has been commissioned by National Museums Liverpool, together with the Liverpool Culture Company and Professor Phil Redmond CBE and Mrs Alexis Redmond. Others who have supported the commission are David M. Robinson Ltd, Liverpool Vision, Northwest Regional Development Agency, Ethel Austin Property Group, Barbara A. McVey, Rensburg Sheppards Investment Management.

The exhibition 'Ben Johnson's Liverpool Cityscape 2008 and the World Panorama Series' has been sponsored by the University of Liverpool.

Photo credits

Pages 36–37, 39, 52: Hugh Gilbert
Pages 4, 5, 57: Prudence Cumming Associates
Additional photography: Ben Johnson,
Richard Gibson, Ann Bukantas, Clare Bates

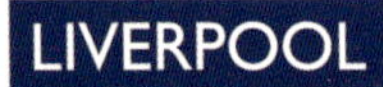

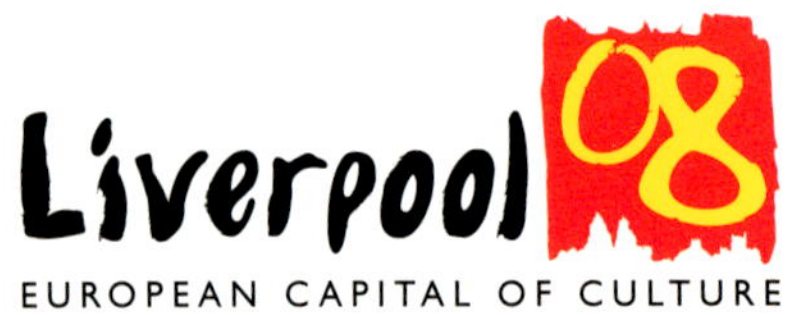

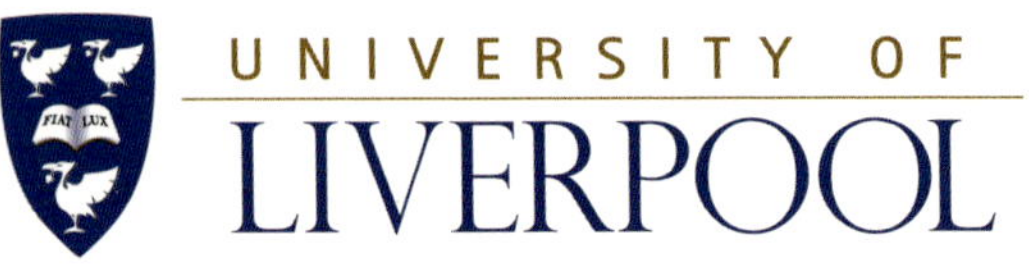

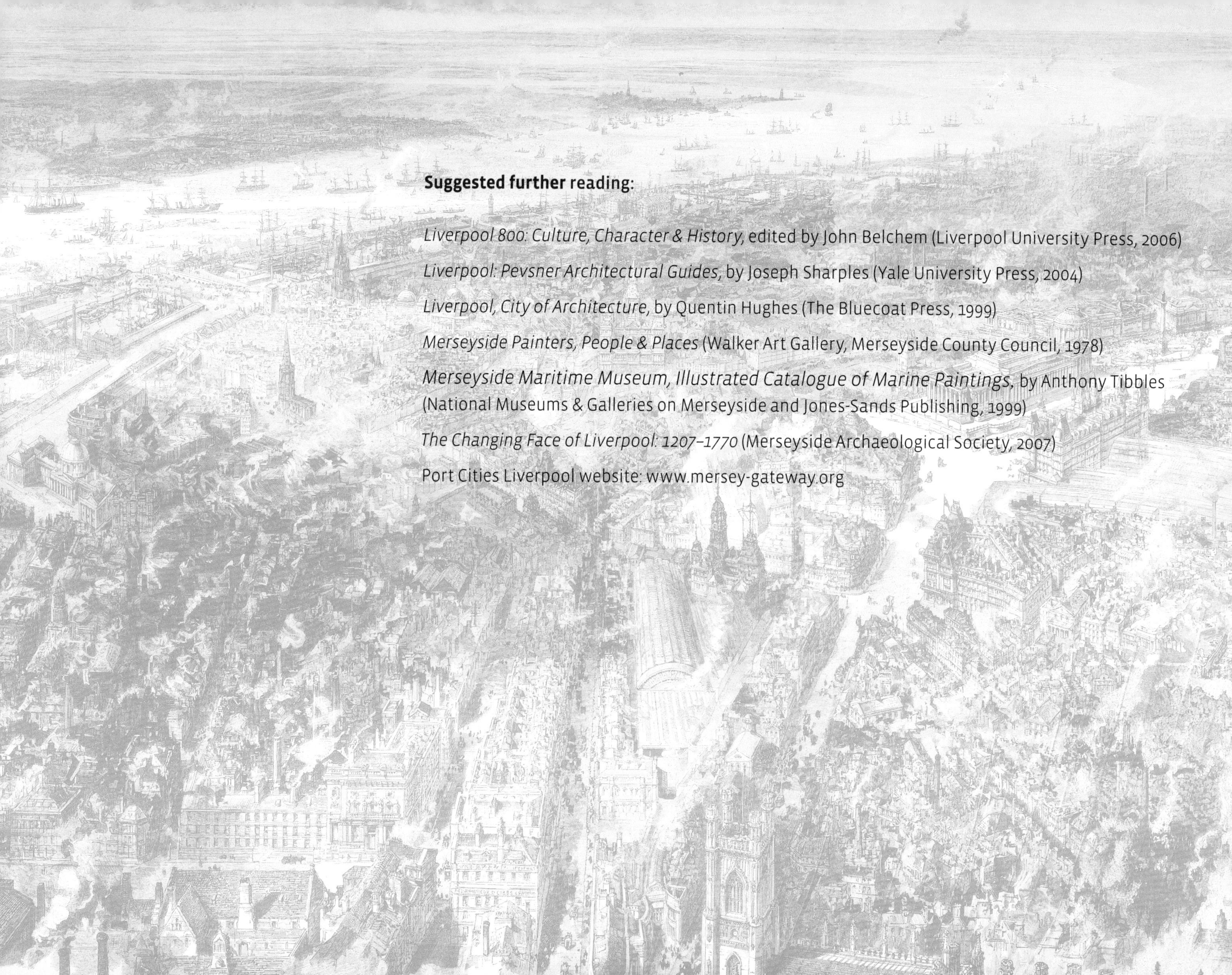

Suggested further reading:

Liverpool 800: Culture, Character & History, edited by John Belchem (Liverpool University Press, 2006)

Liverpool: Pevsner Architectural Guides, by Joseph Sharples (Yale University Press, 2004)

Liverpool, City of Architecture, by Quentin Hughes (The Bluecoat Press, 1999)

Merseyside Painters, People & Places (Walker Art Gallery, Merseyside County Council, 1978)

Merseyside Maritime Museum, Illustrated Catalogue of Marine Paintings, by Anthony Tibbles (National Museums & Galleries on Merseyside and Jones-Sands Publishing, 1999)

The Changing Face of Liverpool: 1207–1770 (Merseyside Archaeological Society, 2007)

Port Cities Liverpool website: www.mersey-gateway.org

Ben Johnson

Ben Johnson was born in Llandudno, North Wales in 1946. He studied at the Royal College of Art, London. His first solo exhibition was held in New York in 1969, and since then he has shown widely in Britain (including twice at the John Moores exhibitions of contemporary painting at the Walker Art Gallery, Liverpool) and worldwide. He was made an honorary Fellow of the Royal Institute of British Architects in 1990, the only contemporary painter to be so honoured, for his contribution to the public understanding of contemporary architecture.

Ann Bukantas is Curator of Fine Art at National Museums Liverpool.